Toward Tomorrow

Toward Tomorrow

New Visions for General Music

Sandra L. Stauffer, Editor

MUSIC EDUCATORS NATIONAL CONFERENCE

Contents

Section 3   Reflections and Applications

Introduction

In 1980, the Society for General Music was established to provide a forum for general music educators within the Music Educators National Conference. Ironically, the founding of SGM coincided with the beginning of a new cycle of educational reform. The National Commission on Excellence in Education was created in 1981, and the Commission's report, *A Nation at Risk: The Imperative for Educational Reform,* was released in 1983. *Soundings,* a newsletter publication of the Society for General Music, was first printed in 1981 and was replaced in 1987 by *General Music Today.* One year later, Charles Fowler's *Can We Rescue the Arts for America's Children?* refocused the debate about the role and place of the arts in the nation's schools. In 1991, when the Bush administration published *America 2000: An Education Strategy,* columns in *General Music Today* covered every level of education from preschool through adulthood, and articles addressed evaluation in general music, views of principals and classroom teachers, and general music educators' roles in educating the rest of the education community about the arts.

Growing concern about the place of music in the schools of the twenty-first century, however, and about the role of general music in the curriculum led members of the Society for General Music and MENC to plan a symposium. Titled *Toward Tomorrow: New Visions for General Music,* the symposium was held in Reston, Virginia, in October 1993. For three days, more than two hundred music educators and other symposium participants considered the future of general music, heeding, perhaps, a call similar to that of an ancient prophet who warned, "Where there is no vision, the people perish."

Section 1

Looking toward Tomorrow

Creating a new vision for general music requires consideration of the larger social and educational contexts in which music education occurs. The perceptions of constituencies within the education community, the music profession, and our society affect music education programs both directly and indirectly. The following five articles, by the symposium plenary session speakers, provide different lenses through which to view the context and role of music education in the schools of tomorrow. Gene R. Carter writes from the perspective of the general education community and from his experience as a teacher, administrator, and executive director of the Association for Supervision and Curriculum Development. Jane M. Healy, author and teacher, provides thoughts from education, psychology, and brain research. Charles Fowler supplies the perspective of a writer, educator, and philosopher in the arts, particularly music. Morton Subotnick adds the thinking and commentary of a professional musician and composer. Sally Monsour voices the perspective of general music educators. All five authors encourage connections and new ways of thinking about the future of schools and of music education.

Creating a new vision for music education requires consideration of the changing nature of schools. Gene R. Carter, executive director of the Association for Supervision and Curriculum Development, considers the continuous process of educational transformation. Schools of the future, he notes, will not be captive to the linear thinking and models of the past, but will instead be places in which compelling new images of education offer rich, diverse, and challenging opportunities for students and teachers. If we are willing to learn to see the world anew, this future is ours to create.

Schools of Tomorrow

By Gene R. Carter

Ralph Waldo Emerson wrote about life as an ongoing encounter with the unknown and created this image: "We wake and find ourselves on a stair; there are stairs below us which we seem to have ascended, there are stairs above us ... which go out of sight."

The world in which we live and will live and the environment in which schools operate are without precedent. This is not a profound revelation; however, although many of the elements have remained the same, the pace and complexity of changes to new forms, ways of living, and values are of an order of magnitude never before experienced.

In this last decade of the twentieth century, we are at the beginning of a time of transformational change in the ways that teaching, learning, and schooling are conceived and implemented. With the multitude of issues, challenges, and opportunities that confront us these days, it seems more imperative that we take time to create new realities.

Our journey into the schools of tomorrow requires that we open our minds and hearts to the dynamic and compelling new images, new constructs, new understandings, and new language of educational transformation.

One hundred years ago, our nation's wealth was based on raw materials. Fifty years ago, it was based on the huge capacity we had for mass production. Today, it's based on what people know and what they can learn. Today, education still is the great equalizer. It is also, however, the great energizer, as well as the best change agent we can possibly have.

America's schools have been the cornerstones of progress for more than two centuries—we have seen what education can do. But it is also instructive to remember that it's only been in the last half century that America fully established a unitary, universal system of public education offering twelve years of free schooling to all children in every state.

As we move toward the year 2000, the educational system's ability to foster lifelong learning will be seen as our single most important route to personal fulfillment, better citizenship, and a higher standard of living. That is why we must make sure that our schools are ready for the twenty-first century.

Tomorrow's leaders must reject the event-driven approach and substitute a value-driven approach to creating a preferred future. We owe it to ourselves and the children we serve to cast

Gene R. Carter is executive director of the Association for Supervision and Curriculum Development in Alexandria, Virginia.

off outdated concepts of leadership and move into the future with passion and confidence, embracing a leadership stance that enables educators and students alike to reach their potential.

To confront a world where the rules change daily will require leaders who are not captive to the past. We must let go of the way things have been done. The leaders of the new world will be those who see a different world and realize they must also change to help others get there.

"To be responsible inventors and discoverers, we need the courage to relinquish most of what we have cherished, to abandon our interpretations about what does and doesn't work." As Einstein advised, "No problem can be solved from the same consciousness that created it. We must learn to see the world anew."

In the past we had a love affair with linear systems. We managed by separating things into discrete entities. We constructed walls and boundaries; we fragmented our learning, our schools, and our world. We broke knowledge into disciplines and subjects. We focused on predictive models of human behavior.

Think for a moment about some of the characteristics of the typical school of the past:

■ It was self-contained, isolated, and unconnected.

■ Time was constrained in blocks, courses, coverage, and competition.

■ There was conversation but little dialogue—the talk was dominated by teachers.

■ Learning was dispensed information, not constructed meaning.

■ Learning was defined by the calendar, not by performance.

■ Coverage and reproduction were more important than understanding and meaning.

■ Concept segmentation was more highly valued than concept integration.

■ Competition in learning was a more powerful motivator than collaboration.

While there is no blueprint for the school of tomorrow, a consensus is emerging that a good school is one focused on the heart of the educational enterprise—the classroom. Futurists envision the school as a place where the focus is on the classroom and the students. In the schools of tomorrow the notion of school as a place with four walls and with a bell at the beginning and end of the day will be gone.

In the schools that many futurists envision, understanding and intellect will be as valued as athletics are today. Students will become more active learners who assume an increased responsibility for their own education. The emphasis will be on applying and using knowledge to solve real-world problems, not just on regurgitating facts. And the traditional walls between education and the broader community will come tumbling down.

In such schools all students will be expected to meet higher standards regarding what they know and can do. And the vision of what a successful high school graduate should be will drive both the curriculum and assessments.

Students will be active participants in the teaching and learning process. Schools will focus on performance, where children are doing things, not just watching someone else. In the past, the biggest performer in too many classrooms has been the teacher.

These schools will be communities of learners in which as much attention is paid to the intellectual and developmental needs of adults as of children. The intellectual development of teachers and that of their students go hand in hand. The focus will be on raising the standards and expectations for all students, not just the college bound. The new conventional wisdom is that, in the future, all students will have to learn to think for a living.

Exactly what world-class standards are and who should set them is the object of an intense and often acrimonious debate. But there is little disagreement that schools will need to focus more on student outcomes than they have in the past, and that those outcomes should be sufficiently rich and challenging to engage all students.

Any school's plan for the future must include designing research-based interventions to improve student achievement on significant outcomes. Schools must ensure that everyone has equal access to knowledge if they are to sustain clear and high expectations for all students.

The twenty-first century will discover about teachers what teachers learned about students in the twentieth century: one size doesn't fit all. Just as there are different ways to learn, there are different ways to guide learning. People learn by discovery—by doing, by building, by creating. Teachers will be there to help people learn to ask the right questions. To help them learn where and how to find answers. To guide them in applying knowledge.

Most of all, teachers must have the time and opportunity to learn from each other and to take risks together. In most schools today, teachers rarely have the chance to catch their breath, let alone engage in reflection or self-rejuvenation. In the future, at the very least, we must imagine schools in which teachers are in frequent conversation with each other about their work, have easy and necessary access to each other's classrooms, take it for granted that they should comment on each other's work, and have the time to develop common standards for their work and that of their students.

Schools that have engaged in futures planning invariably come to the conclusion that character development and civic competence are essential because of the diminished importance of many traditional institutions in the lives of today's youth. Parents, teachers, and communities are concerned that children develop good character. Students must develop values to guide them in applying what they have learned in school. Additionally, Henry Huffman notes that the school must have a positive ethos in order to foster good character. He adds that "we must reach for new standards of character for our children." Schools must play a pivotal role in the preparation of a proactive, sensitive citizenry that can meet the challenges of the new century.

Technology has transformed the workplace significantly. In most cases, technology use in schools has not kept pace with changes in business or industry. Teachers tend to use technology to do the same jobs they've always done, except more vividly, more quickly, and in greater quantities. The power of technology to transform the workplace is still largely unrealized in schools. Transformation will not occur unless technology is permitted to change the way teachers teach and the way students learn.

We must alter the current instructional paradigm to reflect what we know about how children learn. Robert Marzano tells us that the process of learning involves the interaction of five types of learning:

1. Positive attitudes and perceptions about learning.

2. Thinking involved in acquiring and integrating knowledge.

3. Thinking involved in using knowledge meaningfully.

4. Thinking involved in extending and refining knowledge.

5. Productive habits of mind.

The challenge for educators is to bring about a fundamental shift in the way we think about the purpose of teaching and learning. The school is not now a learning organization. Irregular waves of change, episodic projects, fragmentation of effort, and grinding overload is the lot of most schools.

We must create learning communities that:

■ Foster interactive and collaborative approaches to learning;

■ Encourage interdisciplinary connections and understandings;

■ Provide a forum for risk-taking, experimentation, and active hands-on learning; and

■ Provide a social setting that values and promotes individual achievement and fosters ethical and moral decision making.

As we move forth to prepare our students for the new millennium—for a world of work and service that we can hardly comprehend—perhaps we need to connect more closely to our aesthetic and intellectual side, which links us with the higher strands of the great cultures, and with one another, and with ourselves.

Additionally, we should heed the admonition of Elliot Eisner that "artistic tasks, unlike so much of what is now taught in schools, develop the ability to judge, to assess, to experience a wide range of meanings that exceed what we are able to say in words. The limits of language are not the limits of our consciousness."

Changing our habits of mind and heart will enable us to create a more integrative, holistic, and systemic vision of the world and this will flow naturally into a new vision of schools of tomorrow: Schools that enable children and adults to find greater intellectual and social coherence in what they learn, that enable them to interact freely with information of all kinds, and that foster connections and integration. Clearly, the challenge is to move away from a system with little clarity of purpose toward a system drawn into the future by a compelling vision of what we can achieve in our schools and our communities.

I want to thank all of you who teach and guide our children, staff our schools, lead our communities, and build our future. And I want to thank you most of all for your clear and profound devotion to the work of teaching and learning.

Norman Lear once said that "all journeys are filled with pot holes and mines, but the only way we can move beyond them is to approach them and recognize them for what they are. Everywhere you trip is where the treasure lies."

And the treasure is indeed ours to uncover.

Jane M. Healy, author of Endangered Minds: Why Children Don't Think and What We Can Do About It, *examines the problems and possibilities of tomorrow's learners. Environments in which children learn and grow impact neurophysiological development in powerful ways, resulting in changed habits of mind and ways of thinking. Multimodal, highly participatory experiences provided in music classes, Healy believes, may enhance neurophysiological integration important to the development of critical mental skills. Music may indeed be essential to growing brains.*

Musical Brains for the World of Tomorrow

By Jane M. Healy

I am especially delighted to address you, the educators of tomorrow's creators, practitioners, patrons, and consumers of the musical arts. I applaud you for your vitality and flexibility in devoting serious consideration to music education for a new century. Personally, I believe making music and appreciating it have enormous brain-building potential too long overlooked by educators. In fact, if we teach music well, we may help our learners of tomorrow integrate—at a neurophysiological level—the mental skills and habits essential for the next century.

Because our eldest son is a professional musician, I have done some firsthand observing and speculating about music's effects on the growing brain. First, it seems obvious that both skilled musicianship and sophisticated appreciation of music require special types of experiences and learning as well as innate ability—an interaction, if you will, between gift and grit. Talent must be augmented by disciplined attention and preparation; emotional and aesthetic appreciation need refinement by critical analysis. If taught properly,

Jane M. Healy is a learning specialist at the Vail Mountain School in Vail, Colorado, and holds an appointment as adjunct assistant professor at Cleveland State University.

these skills may have integrative effects on the developing nervous system.

What we are basically talking about is a dynamic synergy between holistic and analytic thought—a splendid example of effective interaction between the analytic and sequential skills of the left hemisphere (that is, musical notation, timing, sequencing) and the more holistic ones of the right (that is, melody, emotional tone, the "shape" or interpersonal effectiveness of a composition or a performance). Music also pulls simultaneously on sensory functions from the back of the cortex and the executive analyzer and planner in the frontal sections. Not to mention the limbic system, which is the primary locus of emotion, motivation, and memory, where music has its most powerful roots and effects. Needless to say, this latter dimension of the system has been sadly neglected in traditional school curricula. (Yes, so-called "whole-brain" learning is much more complicated than most of us have been told—but music taps it all.)

What type of climate in music classrooms will enable the learners of tomorrow—either as makers or appreciators of music—to develop and realize this critical synthesis of diverse mental abilities and emotional response? Who, in fact, will be the learners of tomorrow, and how do we best reach and teach them? Here's the critical question: Will they be new brains for a new century or will they be just like children of today with the same developmental needs? My answer to the above is that they will have new ways of learning, but they will still be children.

Much that is critical about childhood and, in fact, about creating and learning, will not change in any generation. The importance of mental habits—personal caring and the desire to create, coupled with the internal discipline to start and complete a project, critical judgment exercised along the way, and the self-assurance to implement a project—will doubtless survive the test of technology, cyberspace, hypertext, or whatever the year 2000 can conjure up. Yet these gifts, required for competent, much less inspired, participation in any field, do not leap automatically into every child's brain; they take time, need models, and require nurturance. Nor are they simply a matter of the genetic draw, for the environment is a major factor in maximizing or blunting innate potential.

Intelligent response to music, as to any creative work, demands specialized skills and experiences in which caring adults provide the raw material (for example, trips to children's concerts, playing good music in the home) while modeling habits of selectivity and appreciation. It is no surprise that researchers and experienced parents agree unequivocally that what we show children in our own behavior is retained and incorporated far better than anything we tell them (sometimes to our lasting mortification).

In my book, *Endangered Minds,* I have highlighted some concerns about the environments that are preparing these learners of the future and about the physical substructures of their brains. Our children do not often have time, freedom to play and create, or experiences of rising successfully to a challenge. They also do not often have a framework of support from competent adults. These needs are the same whether it is the year 1200 or 2200.

Please consider: a paucity of close relationships with positive adult role models; a fast-paced, violent, emotionally threatening (or deadening) media culture; a prevalent cynicism about quality and taste; a rushed society bent on

product at the expense of process, with a resulting disrespect for both childhood and learning; and the presence of technology that we have not as yet learned to utilize in developmentally appropriate ways for children.

On the other hand, the media and technology are changing the picture and the learners. They offer potentially exciting benefits in shaping both brains and learning environments for the learners of tomorrow.

Environments Shape Children's Brains

Many experienced teachers report recent environmental "habits-of-mind" changes that impinge heavily on music classes:

■ Attention: There is a rising incidence of "attention deficit disorder."

■ Analytic/critical listening: Our children are bombarded by noise, so they learn early to tune out. Many may even have suffered ear damage. Studies of experimental rats show too much harsh noise can create emotional disturbances and violent antisocial behavior as well as attention problems. Even prenatally, infants object to overly loud music.

■ Language and "inner speech": Do we give our children an opportunity to hear their inner musical voices?

■ Creativity: Open-ended thinking is one concern—today's kindergartners reenact Mighty Morphin scripts instead of developing creative play. And discipline and "stick-to-it-iveness" (or vigilance) is another concern. These qualities can easily be reduced by fast-paced television formats that give instant gratification.

■ Time: Children have a lack of time, which is needed to ponder, experiment, and play.

■ Visualization: Television provides ready-made images and less-active mental processing. Does it thus limit the growth of connections between right and left hemispheres? What are we sacrificing by plunging young children into abstract-symbolic video or computer worlds without the concrete foundations for language, imagery, and abstract thought?

■ Rhythm: Many children are starved for

touch and body movement. A prevalence of heavy "beat" may replace internal rhythm gained from personally generated experience.

> It's the nature of the music they're listening to, this popular music. It is different from other kinds of music in that the tempo is exactly like a metronome: beat, beat, beat. Studies have shown that flashing lights at a fixed frequency (flash, flash, flash) sets up a rhythm in the brain that interferes with normal processing. The same may be true of the auditory system. ... My own feeling is that you're going to make kids space out because it's putting the brain into a loop: it can't desynchronize and therefore you're really blocking the capacity for thinking.—*Dr. Jerre Levy (University of Chicago), quoted in* Endangered Minds

Tomorrow's Learners in the Classroom

While many of us doubtless wish we could change some aspects of this culture, let's not hold our breath! The good news is that today's children, as you doubtless realize, have great potential—possibly even to shove human social evolution into entire new realms of creativity and thought. Meanwhile, however, I believe we as educators are going to have to take over many of the functions that have traditionally been performed by the culture—and the earlier the better, while brains are still at their most malleable.

Tomorrow's learners will have the same basic developmental needs as today's, but we may have to do a better job of addressing them, since the outside culture is giving us so little support. Here are a few obvious suggestions for music pedagogy, which I trust will at least confirm your own good instincts:

1. Clearly, it is essential to give children extensive experience in pleasant, participatory activities with melody, rhythm, and listening games—getting them at age two or three if possible, and extending these experiences longer than we might previously have expected to. For a generation of watchers, integrated experiences in body movement are essential. The motor cortex, which controls planning, organizing, and monitoring sequential body movement, is directly associated with the parts of the brain that direct the same skills in singing, composing, playing an instrument, or mentally anticipating and sequencing any intellectual activity. This hands-on involvement should, in turn, increase motivation and task orientation—factors too often missing in worksheet-driven classroom curricula. Many of today's children have also lacked sufficient fine-motor hand exercise to enable either effortless handwriting or the fingering of an instrument; these skills should be developed before formal instruction if pleasurable learning and success are expected. (Incidentally, snapping Lego blocks together doesn't seem to serve the same purpose; children also need practice with a variety of fine-motor sequences.)

2. Children who have been embedded in a largely symbolic video and computer society may have bypassed many of the essential play and social explorations that underlie more advanced levels of conceptualization in any field. Therefore, I would hold back on abstract-symbolic input (musical notation, for example) in favor of more personally meaningful experiences and cooperative group activities. Even at best, most brains are not ready to combine across modalities (that is, look at the notes and sing the melody or play the keys) until *at least* age seven; for many children this development occurs much later.

Clearly this is a strong, brain-based rationale for programs such as Dalcroze and Orff; There are, of course, many others that would fit the bill. Real-life motor and instrumental activities may be especially important to ground children who will, as adults, have leisure choices of "virtual" as well as "real" reality (the ultimate redundancy), and who may be unable to distinguish acoustic from synthesized music if they have never learned to appreciate the difference.

3. Tomorrow's learners will need to be critical consumers of visual as well as auditory input, because much information processing as well as entertainment at home, school, and in the work place will take place in front of a screen. Experiences combining these modalities (for

example, creating a video to go with a song; analyzing and discussing visual presentations of music, and so on) build skills requisite for any kind of sophisticated response to new multimedia cultural forms that will doubtless emerge in the twenty-first century. Since many young children come to school nowadays without the auditory basics, such as nursery rhymes that provide experiences in linking rhythm and language, spontaneous integration of music and language become even more vital. For older students, critical analysis of rock videos is an interesting avenue, if you can handle it.

4. Music intrinsically appeals to the emotional brain, or limbic system, which lies at the root of motivation and many forms of memory. By failing to infuse music (and the visual arts as well) more thoroughly into the entire curriculum, we have lost enormous instructional potential, not only to enhance conceptual learning, but even for rote-level memory tasks, such as making up original tunes for the multiplication tables. Children with divergent learning styles or attention deficit disorders would be most likely to profit from such interdisciplinary expansion. Doubtless you wish the schools would wake up to this message; I would suggest that as problems in the classroom multiply, they may soon be ready to hear it.

5. Music teachers should all be experts in building critical listening skills. I would like to see music teachers all greatly in demand as consultants to classroom teachers because of their expertise in teaching children to be good listeners—to language as well as to music. If music teachers have not developed an armamentarium of effective listening games and exercises, why not make it a major professional goal? It is certainly needed, as the audiences of the future are in your capable hands.

6. Today's students (the "you deserve a break today" crowd) are well trained as critical consumers and tend to reject products appearing to lack relevance to their personal lives. Music should be an easy "sell"; for example, comparing rap with Rossini, a music video with Mussorgsky, and so on.

7. One constant, in any era, is the need to anchor instruction in children's developmental needs at different ages. As with all good teaching, we need to avoid overly abstract material, the memorizing of lengthy new vocabulary, or too many pencil-and-paper tests until most learners reach formal operational thinking at around age eleven to sixteen. Brains differ markedly in this respect, and formal abstract thought appears to be domain-specific: that is, one might be a formal thinker in verbal concepts, but not in musical ones, and vice versa. Of course, gifted musical brains need different sorts of stimulation, but for the general classroom, keep it interesting, keep the kids actively engaged, and make it somehow relevant to their perceived needs or experiences. I would hate to see music classes conducted in the manner described by a recent critic of education in general: like going to the best restaurant in the world and being fed the menu.

8. Is it too much to hope that we may be able to exert some sort of influence on the media makers to improve the quality of kids' television programs? Television is a powerful teaching tool, and we have a generation of children who are musically literate for all the songs on "Sesame Street," but who have a poor base for appreciation of broader forms. Why not give them some elementary grounding in Mozart—or other worthwhile foundations—as well? Some interesting new research has suggested that perfect pitch is partially acquired by the brain as a result of high-quality musical input during an as yet undefined critical period early in life. In other words, the basic potential must be there, but the environment actually makes it happen. If so, early musical experiences take on an entirely new importance.

Minds of the Future?

Finally, let me briefly address the unknown potential of tomorrow's learners to move us into new forms of thought and creativity. While I was in the process of writing *Endangered Minds,* I talked to thousands of teachers who lamented significant recent changes in children's mental habits. By the time I reached chapter twelve, it occurred to me that nature must be giving us a message about the future. Perhaps our hyperactive multitaskers who can focus on several things at once, for example, are developing highly adaptive skills for a technological age. We may well be on the cusp of a change in the way the human brain processes information, and intellectual skills may need to change along with new forms of literacy and, doubtless, of artistry as well.

Certainly, it appears that linear analysis—of language, of musical notation, and of auditory input of any type—is yielding to much more visual, holistic, emotionally driven forms of processing. This apparent ceding of neural real estate from the left hemisphere is troubling to me as a reader, writer, and analytic thinker. I believe we must fight to preserve these critical, albeit old-fashioned, skills in the minds of our children. It is, however, likely that other, perhaps right hemisphere–type, skills will be more highly prized in a society where three-dimensional computer models are a major form of

information transmission. Since many musical brains are extremely talented in these respects, the future looks bright. Without belaboring this point, let me suggest first that we appreciate the students of today—who point the way to the learners of tomorrow—and second that we remind ourselves that these children still are and will continue to be children, but with different needs from those for whom old approaches used to work. As we use our own creative skills to envision new curricula and methods, let us try to incorporate what is best of the old in our visions of the new. I hope we can somehow instill critical listening and analysis, sustained interest in a project, and the ability to tolerate frustration and keep trying, along with open-mindedness to new forms and imaginations.

You educators have the awesome responsibility of shaping the musical brains—and the societal attitudes—of those who will make, select, and financially support music in the next generation. It is in your hands to preserve the best of the old while accepting the challenges of the new. I wish you well—for your individual joy, and for our cultural future.

"Our future is in our own hands," states Charles Fowler in his challenge to music educators to rethink and reframe what they do. Fowler, writer and thinker in the arts, criticizes the profession's tendency to overspecialize and to separate the aesthetic experience from human concerns. He advocates reconnecting music education with general education, social purposes, and American culture. "By thinking differently about music education," he believes, "we can control our own destiny."

Arts Education for Tomorrow
Straight Talk about the Future of Music Education

By Charles Fowler

I was surprised to be asked to speak on the future of arts education, since I have absolutely no credentials as a soothsayer. What I do have is an enormous concern for this field and an unwavering belief in its possibilities and its value. Like most of you, I have been deeply concerned about the increasingly tangential position of music within the curriculum of American schools. Music education is in serious trouble, and I'm not certain we have a plan to deal with it. I think we have to recognize that our future is in our own hands and that what we do today will determine in large measure what tomorrow will be. And I have to admit that thought gives me qualms.

Music education, overall, has been in a state of serious decline for almost three decades. At every level, we seem to have all the status of a third-world country. We could certainly draw that conclusion from the results of Charles Leonhard's 1991 survey of the arts in public schools, in which he compared statistics gathered by the National Education Association in 1962 with our situation in 1989—a period of almost thirty years. During that time he found that the minutes allotted to general music in grades 1–3 decreased by 25 percent; in large schools the time dropped more than 29 percent, from seventy-five minutes per week in 1962 to fifty-three minutes per week in 1989. In grades 4–6, there was a 22 percent loss. Music offerings in secondary schools have "decreased markedly."[1] Whereas general music was offered in 43.6 percent of secondary schools in 1962, it is offered in only 22.3 percent of large high schools today, a drop of 51 percent. Instrumental instruction has declined severely: 30 percent in wind and percussion and 40 percent in strings. These declines in music education during the past thirty years do not bode well for the future. (See figure 1.)

Why have we suffered these severe reductions? We are experts at making excuses. We regularly point out that the reform movement, begun in 1983 with the publication of *A Nation at Risk*,[2] omitted the arts. Then we claim, with some justification, that the public does not understand us or the value of what we do. And

© *1995 by Charles Fowler. Charles Fowler is director of National Cultural Resources, Inc., and a Washington, D.C.-based arts writer, speaker, consultant, and advocate. He is author of* Can We Rescue the Arts for America's Children? *(American Council for the Arts, 1988), the high school textbook,* Music! Its Role and Importance in Our Lives *(Glencoe/Macmillan/McGraw-Hill, 1994), and* Strong Arts, Strong Schools *(in press: Oxford University Press).*

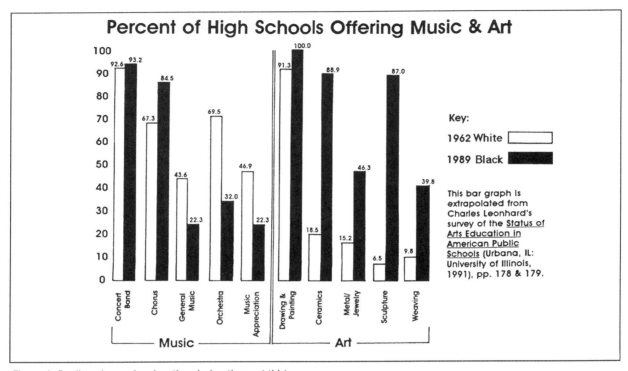

Figure 1. Declines in music education during the past thirty years.

we refer to all those pressures on the curriculum to raise the sagging scores in mathematics and science to compete with foreign students.

All this "logic" might explain the difficulties we face except for one fact: during the same period that music programs have suffered accumulating curtailments in every area on every level, the offerings in visual arts have generally improved. On the elementary level today, even though there have been comparable reductions in the number of minutes allotted to art, Leonhard found that schools are much more likely to offer art and to have a written curriculum for art, and he tells us that visual arts in the secondary schools have "undergone tremendous growth."[3] Drawing and painting are now offered in upwards of 100 percent of schools. Whereas ceramics was offered in only 18.5 percent of secondary schools in 1962, it is offered in 88.9 percent in 1989. Sculpture has risen from 15.2 percent to 46.3 percent of schools, metal/jewelry from 15.2 percent to 46.3 percent, and weaving from 9.8 percent to 39.8 per-

cent. The percentage of secondary schools requiring art has increased dramatically from 6.4 percent in 1962 to 34.3 percent in 1989. In contrast, there has been only a slight increase in the percentage of secondary school that have a music requirement—from 12.9 percent in 1962 to 14.7 percent in 1989. Leonhard concludes: "In 1989 students had access to a level of richness and variety in art experience and learning that may have been almost inconceivable in 1962."[4]

I do not convey this data to make us envy art, but rather to show that during the same years music suffered severe decline, visual art education managed to markedly expand and improve its offerings. Why has music declined and art flourished? Part of the answer may be the ferment of the Discipline-Based Art Education (DBAE) movement and the decade-long efforts of the Getty Center for Education in the Arts to improve instruction in visual arts, which has helped bring greater recognition and credibility to art education. But I think something else is apparent here: Our educational climate is not hostile to the arts but pointedly skeptical about the educational significance of music. If this is the case, continuing our present practices may be consigning music to self-annihilation. What options do we have? What can we do to reestablish, irrefutably, the educational credibility of music? If change is called for, can we manage to get our teachers to alter their ways?

One thing is certain: The education world that we are a tenuous part of does not put any priority on reforming arts education, even though it might agree that arts education needs reforming. There are more urgent priorities. So if we are going to create a better tomorrow for music, we will have to do it ourselves. Will inclusion of the arts in the Goals 2000: Educate America Act, the establishment of the National Standards, and the support of the current secretary of education solve our difficulties? They will help us, but I am convinced that we have to operate on our own problems if we are going to reverse the current trends.

My own search for answers started six years ago when I decided to take on the enormous task of creating a new approach for general music at the high school level. That set me to thinking about our needs, the changing landscape of our musical culture, and the condition of music education and how we might improve it. I started by asking some very basic questions: What are our problems? What are we doing that might be defeating us? What can we do—what must we do—to better ourselves? I was determined to come up with a different approach—one that would put music back solidly in the high school curriculum.

In pondering our state and our future, it seemed to me that music education had become disconnected from the school and the society it was supposed to serve. It seemed reasonable, then, that music education needed to reassert some basic connections—with general education, with its social purposes, with American culture, and, ultimately, with its own value. I want to explore these connections with you in the next subsections.

Reconnect Music with General Education

Oddly enough, it is often our own teachers who have consigned music to the educational sidelines, presenting it as a special program for the talented or as career education for the few. At MENC's National Biennial In-Service Conference in 1992, an outstanding high school choral director told me, "I'll never use your new textbook. What could make me want to try to reach all those other students? I have a difficult enough time dealing with my choral students. Besides, what would I have to give up to put a general course in place?" I'm going to try to respond to her very real concerns.

This same teacher, over the years, has complained about the lack of status accorded music in her school. I believe there is a direct connection between our selectivity and our status. As long as music in secondary schools continues to be presented as a special study for the talented, it consigns itself to the fringes of educational respectability and necessity.

The entire music curriculum has only one justification—general education. This is a change in thinking that must permeate the profession: not to see ourselves just as conductors and directors, but first as educators. In this sense, our increasing emphasis of specialization—whether as a choral or band director or as a jazz or Orff educator—have caused us to lose the precious perspective of the generalist. Teaching music in public schools is not about being a conductor. It is not about teaching technical competence, but, rather, it's about understanding—both human and musical. If our intent is to establish music as basic education, then everything we do in schools must illuminate the necessity of music and its educational value for all people. We need to get back to first principles.

We must face the fact that musical performance groups, no matter how good, have not legitimized music education as a basic or won it an undisputed place in the core curriculum of American schools. And if we are not basic in today's schools, we are peripheral—or dead. Music education is conducted today as if it were its own singular, isolated enterprise, disconnected from American society and even from mainline education. Kids may play twenty or more marches while they are in the school band but have no idea how a march is structured or how the march, the band, or music serve our society. This doesn't mean we should give up performance or deemphasize it or stop offering electives. It means we must treat the performance experience as a part of general education and use our performing groups to get at the core of how music serves human needs. Why learn to play a musical instrument? David Elliott's work is helping us to better understand the insights and attributes humans acquire in the process of mastering an instrument and learning how to perform together.[5]

Over the years, the development of musical skills has narrowed the focus of music education, and our teachers have abnegated their responsibility to general education. People rightly ask why young people should learn to play instruments and sing, to read musical notation, to compose and arrange, to make critical judgments about music, or to study any number of other aspects of music. What makes these goals educational? Why are they important? We have become masters at teaching what Elliot Eisner calls "disembodied knowledge." We teach music as if it has no relationship whatever to the rest of education, to people, to society, to the times, or to the circumstances and needs of our world. The content of most music education programs appears to be irrelevant to basic education. We have neglected to make clear and explicit the connections between music and life that make art personally significant and meaningful.

I believe that we need to regeneralize music education in all its aspects and that a reemphasis on general education is the key to our recovery. The primary aim of our performing groups is general education, not concerts and contest ratings. Technique, after all, is a vehicle to convey musical meaning, not an end in itself. At every level, providing educational opportunities for every student is the foundation of the music education program. By reaching out to all secondary students, we position music as an essential part of basic education and we gain educational status.

Reconnect Music with Its Social Purposes

Pablo Casals, the great cellist, said, "Music must serve a purpose; it must be a part of something larger than itself, a part of humanity ...."[6] Expert teachers build connections. They skillfully link their students with the subject matter at hand, and they make certain that students see how that subject matter relates significantly with their own lives and with the real world around them. They establish relationships between the many worlds of the classroom and the many worlds outside.

Building connections is a mechanism good teachers use to help students become self-motivated. These teachers know that such connection making is central to establishing the relevance of what is being learned. In order to assure that their students value the learning enterprise, they help them to relate personally to what they are studying and to see the importance of it to their own lives. We need to make these connections in music.

In the arts, we have made the mistake of teaching technique at the expense of meaning. Skills are developed in isolation. We have tended to separate art-making and art-understanding from life. We are not alone in overstressing the technical aspects and ignoring the purpose. Jacques Barzun points out that "we do not get at the heart of the matter." Consequently, there is no humanizing effect.[7] Only when music is taught as a language, rather than a technical challenge or history, does it have human value. When subjects are not taught as value, literature is reduced to grammar, history to a list of dates, science to a compendium of formulas, and music to a series of techniques. The art itself tends to get lost.

If the new National Standards for Music Education are indicative of how the field views its work and its mission, then, judging by the draft in the September 1993 *Music Educators Journal* (the *National Standards for Arts Education* were published by MENC in 1994), the emphasis is disproportionately on skill development.[8] I think it is also revealing that a fourth category, "The Nature and Value of the Arts," was dropped. Developing technique has been the end-all of music education for as long as I can remember. It is our triumph and our travesty. We assume that because students sing in the choir or play in the band for several years they emerge from school with a respect for music and its importance. That is fallacious thinking. In learning technique there is no guarantee that students will acquire insight into the importance of music. We take that connection for granted, but we do so at our own peril.

Music education is not just about skill development, nor are performing groups just about performance. What good is it to teach students to play and sing the right notes if we don't affect their lives, their outlook, their human understanding? Technique and performance have become ends in themselves but at the expense of establishing the importance of music and its human and cultural functions. We are not merely teachers of technical competence.

Another major factor in our current situation is the condition of the arts in American society. As much as I personally enjoy them, I believe that museums and concert halls have done their arts an enormous and devastating disservice. They have separated art and music from their cultural functions in real life. They have put them on pedestals, removing them from the notion that the arts are of the people, by the people, and for the people. By losing sight of their practical importance, we have consigned the arts to being special and precious and removed them from human priority.

That attitude is reflected in a recent survey of the American public commissioned by the National Cultural Alliance, a coalition of forty-one arts and humanities organizations. It reveals that the vast majority of people tend to be supportive of the arts, but they just do not see much value in them in relation to their own lives.[9] (See figure 2.)

These public attitudes carry over to affect the status of the arts in schools. Parents believe that the arts are nice for their children, but they tend to separate them from the important business of preparation for the real world through the traditional basics, particularly science and mathematics. How do we invade these deeply rooted public beliefs?

I think we must first of all face the fact that

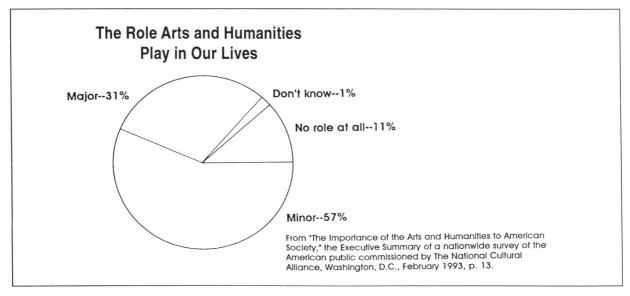

The Role Arts and Humanities Play in Our Lives

Major--31%   Don't know--1%

No role at all--11%

Minor--57%

From "The Importance of the Arts and Humanities to American Society," the Executive Summary of a nationwide survey of the American public commissioned by The National Cultural Alliance, Washington, D.C., February 1993, p. 13.

Figure 2. The attitude of people toward the arts and humanities.

we have not been successful in trying to persuade people of the importance of aesthetic education. That philosophy, important as it has been to us, has tended to aid and abet the prevailing art-for-art's-sake focus of music education. Aesthetic education should be the means, not the end goal, of music education. Bennett Reimer denigrates our intransigent tendency as professionals "to rely on utilitarian panaceas." He says, "Our history is largely one of questing for the 'quick cure.'"[10] But look who we are trying to persuade—school board members, school administrators, and parents, many of whom we left out of our programs. I do not think we have found *any* cure—quick or long term. But it should be painfully clear to us that aesthetic education has not provided a convincing substantiation for music education.

Focusing on our utility is not the problem; the problem is the type of utility we claim. Marcia Milder Outran, professor of philosophy at the University of Minnesota, believes that the aesthetic experience can no longer be separated from areas of human concern. "Even if some [art works] are created to be displayed in museums or concert halls—above and beyond the human fray—many are intended to fill political or religious or moral functions. Their value is diminished, indeed missed, if one ignores this."[11] One of the main aims of music education is to break through public attitudes that view the arts, particularly the classical arts, as elitist, disconnected, and superfluous and to establish the arts as democratic, connected, and essential.

Establishing our utility as a subject is as essential to *our* existence as establishing the value of science is to maintaining *its* status as an educational priority. We have to remember that the whole purpose of arts education is to serve the interests and needs of American youth; that is, the contributions we can make to their lives and their education. But these contributions, and why they are important, have to be made explicit.

We have suggested many practical rationales to justify our educational importance. Yes, let us go right on attempting to accumulate empirical evidence that high-quality arts experiences increase student motivation to learn, school attendance, achievement in basic subjects, creative/critical thinking, self-respect, and parental involvement, and decrease discipline problems, drop-out rates, and student hostility. My own research tells me that these claims have some credibility.[12] But let us first and foremost justify our existence in general education based upon music's primary and indigenous worth—its capacity as a basic form of human communication to help us understand who we are as human beings; to reveal our world as it is and was and might be; to develop our abilities and sensibilities, particularly each human's capacity to excel and to care about other human beings; but most of all, to help us to better understand and live our lives.

Music can teach us humaneness. It can sustain us and soothe us and let us know that we are not alone in feeling as we do. It can provide a compelling link between present and past generations and between present and future generations. It can call our imagination into productive action. As a significant system of human communication, music provides us with a way to record and to share perceptions of the world that would otherwise not be expressible. The arts are truly insightful; they reveal aspects of ourselves and our world that simply cannot be conveyed as well by any other means. Those are incredibly important, but insufficiently represented, dimensions of today's education.

What I am trying to suggest is that music has its own built-in uniqueness that constitutes its raison d'etre. That uniqueness—that type of utilitarianism—should be at the center of our curricula. I am suggesting that we build our curriculum on the solid base of the intrinsic worth of music, not its secondary effects.

Reconnect Music with American Culture

We have been considering ways to reestablish the relevance of music in order to enhance its educational status and save it from educational extinction. Perhaps the most obvious and significant way we can relate to the students and the communities we serve is to explore the relationship of music to the ethnicity of our students. How can, how should, music education relate to the intensifying assertions of ethnicity within the cultural diversity of American civilization? Fifty years ago music education was part of the melting pot, molding students' tastes toward the then-accepted ideal—the traditions of Western art music. Never mind that we did not always succeed in that quest. We zealously pursued the acquisition and elevation of taste as the main goals of music education, and we taught the history of Western art music as one of the main foundations of musical understanding.

We seem now to live in a world of growing factionalism. The human alliances that were forged to combat communism have collapsed into ethnic wars. As the world recoils into smaller and smaller factions and bigotry and hatred thrive in America, we face the ominous prospect that American culture itself is being destabilized. We are becoming a society fragmented into ethnic groups. Arthur M. Schlesinger, Jr., says, "The cult of ethnicity exaggerates differences, intensifies resentment and antagonisms, drives ever deeper the awful wedges between races and nationalities. The endgame is self-pity and self-ghettoization."[13]

The accommodation of diversity, however imperfectly achieved, is central to the ideals of American democracy. But it is a fragile quality that needs constant nurturing and reinforcement. The arts can have an important role in this process, but we have to recognize the pitfalls. Music can function as the glue that binds us to each other; it can also be used as a wedge against social unity. An Afrocentric or Eurocentric curriculum, for example, may promote increased separatism. The term "multicultural" is bantered about frequently today, but I am not certain of its meaning or the effects of its several applications. "Multicultural" is often used to refer only to non-Western, nonwhite cultures. I prefer the terms "intracultural" or "transcultural" because, unlike multicultural, they suggest the interrelationship and interde-

pendence of diverse cultures.

The reason we need to broaden our repertoire and our cultural focus is not just because of the changing demographics of the school and societal population. We need to embrace an intracultural or transcultural perspective because music is one of the fundamental ways that we can develop a sense of social cohesiveness and community—essential social bonds in a society growing evermore divided.

Historian Daniel J. Boorstin says: "The menace to America today is in the emphasis on what separates us rather than on what brings us together—the separations of race, of religious dogma, of religious practice, of origins, of language." He advocates building a sense of community—"an emphasis on what brings us together." He states unequivocally that he "is wary of attempts to create ethnic ghettos. It's an abomination."[14] The arts, particularly music, have an incredibly essential service to provide in bringing our people together. But we have to make certain that arts education functions in this way, not as a survey-smattering of many cultures or as a concentration upon one.

In the arts, how can we reconcile history with multiculturalism? The historical framework limits us to a Western, largely Eurocentric perspective. If African, Asian, and Hispanic music do not fit into a chronological or linear framework, do we therefore ignore these musics or treat them as ancillary exceptions? Are we primarily custodians who guard and transmit only our Anglo-Saxon classical-music past—or some other doctrinaire ethnicity or nationalism? What is our role? Instead, I would like to suggest that we are the guardians of cultural pluralism—a community of disparate musical contributions that belongs to all our citizens. At the same time that it recognizes the European roots of American civilization, the musical legacy of every American encompasses the significant contributions of people of all races.

How do we incorporate this view into our curricula? To fully understand art, we have to consciously reconnect it to its culture and to the purposes it fulfills in its indigenous setting. A sociological, rather than historical, approach can more fairly treat a variety of musical cultures by illuminating their essential role and function in human life. The need to connect music education to community arts enterprises then becomes clear. Cultural sharing becomes the motivation for us to work directly with a variety of community artists, arts organizations, and institutions. This sharing—this cultural exchange—teaches students to recognize and respect the enormous richness of their cultural heritage.

Music offers schools an authentic and compelling vehicle for acquiring transcultural insight and understanding. I believe arts education should stress the individual's right to inclusion not exclusion, and that we should embrace the ideal of a common, though diverse, culture, not a society of restricted ethnic communes. Let us rededicate ourselves to an American creed based on tolerance of differences and on mutual respect. Music provides a powerful and persuasive representation of our diversity and, most important, of our ability to transcend ethnicity and build heterogeneous communities. But the concept of sharing comes with a caveat. We must face the fact that, as David Elliott points out in his essay "Music, Education, and Schooling," "Whatever curricular offerings are perceived to lack universal application are either eliminated or moved to the periphery of the school menu."[15]

How can music education reconnect itself to American culture? By their nature, the arts are diverse representations of human societies and cultural practices. The goal is to tap into diversity as a strength, not try to eliminate it. European culture belongs to Blacks and Asians just as much as jazz, blues, gospel, and soul belong to Anglos. Building respect (not just tolerance) for diverse musical practices is a realistic goal for us and one that establishes for music a critically important educational role. Immediately, music relates to the essential fiber of American society and to one of the important priorities of American education: building bridges between people of different ethnic backgrounds in order to develop and maintain a cohesive American culture. We must keep this goal in front of us.

Value-Centered Music Education

What I have been suggesting here—what I believe from my personal concerns and involvements with music in recent years—is that our curricula should emphasize the value of the arts. According to Paul Lehman, "The unvarnished truth is that if music is not taught, the reason is simply that it is not valued highly enough.... Money is not the real problem. The question is simply one of priorities.[16] I'm suggesting that we take the value question directly into our classrooms, that we teach value. If we want to be certain that we develop a public that understands and values the arts, that is what we should be teaching. We deliberately set out to persuade people—all people—while they are in school and in our classes, not later through our relatively feeble attempts at advocacy. We develop a supportive public by making certain that students leave school with a solid understanding of the role and importance of the arts in their lives.

I am recommending a different paradigm for music education, one that deliberately sets out to reestablish connections with general education, with social purposes, and with our culture—connections that emphasize the importance of music. To increase our stature, I believe we have to reconceptualize our purposes and practices to emphasize value in everything we do, in everything we teach. We never teach just technique or history or repertoire or theory without also teaching *why* they are important. Let us rid the music curriculum of all disembodied knowledge. We never just teach music; we always teach its relationship to people, to purpose, and to meaning. In this way, music deisolates itself, embracing general education in everything we do. In this way, too, we reconnect ourselves to our own essentiality. These connections to value are the essence of music education, the often forgotten other side of the coin. By emphasizing our worth, we take responsibility for our own future and we assure our own survival. I call this new paradigm "value-centered music education."[17]

If music is going to attain the status of a basic, we must demonstrate its educational significance for all students. There just isn't any way around that, and teachers who avoid that truth and refuse to face up to this responsibility are, in effect, defeating themselves and their profession. The public support we crave has to be developed in our classes. It is our first responsibility, and it can't be taken for granted.

I fully believe that we can turn our present circumstances around if we are willing to refocus and readjust. Our problems are not always somebody else's fault. By thinking differently about music education, we can exercise control over our own destiny. We need to reassert the essential role of music in education and in life. In the public schools, everything we do must be recast in the framework of general education, and it is up to us to make certain that our students, administrators, parents, and colleagues understand the worth of music in society and in schools. Whether the vehicle is performance or general music, our determination to contribute to general education is the key to the future of music education.

Notes

1. Charles Leonhard, *The Status of Arts Education in American Public Schools* (University of Illinois: The National Arts Education Research Center, 1991), 178.

2. The National Commission on Excellence in Education, *A Nation at Risk: The Imperative for Educational Reform* (Washington, DC: Department of Education, 1983).

3. Leonhard, *The Status,* 176, 177, and 179.

4. Leonhard, *The Status.*

5. David J. Elliott, "Music as Knowledge," *Journal of Aesthetic Education* 25 (Fall 1991), No. 3.

6. Quoted by Edith Hillman Boxill, "Multicultural Music Therapy: A Global Imperative," *The Newsletter of the American Association for Music Therapy* (Summer 1993), 1.

7. Jacques Barzun, *The Culture We Deserve* (Middletown, CT: Wesleyan University Press, 1989), 110.

8. "National Standards for Arts Education: Music Draft for Member Review," *Music Educators Journal* 80 (September 1993), No. 2. *National Standards for Arts Education* were published by MENC in 1994.

9. "The Importance of the Arts and Humanities to American Society," Executive Summary of a nation-wide survey of the American public (Washington, D.C.: The National Cultural Alliance, February 1993).

10. Bennett Reimer, "Music Education as Aesthetic Education: Past and Present," *Music Educators Journal* 75 (February 1989), No. 6: 26.

11. Quoted in "Discipline-based Art Education and Cultural Diversity," *Newsletter* (The Getty Center for Education in the Arts, Spring 1993): 4.

12. See the study report, "Understanding How the Arts Contribute to Excellent Education" prepared for the National Endowment for the Arts (Philadelphia: Organization & Management Group, Inc., 1991).

13. Arthur M. Schlesinger, Jr., *The Disuniting of America: Reflections on a Multicultural Society* (Knoxville, TN: Whittle Books, 1991), 58.

14. Quoted by Tad Szulc, "The Greatest Danger We Face," *Parade Magazine* (July 25, 1993), 4 and 5.

15. David J. Elliott, "Music, Education and Schooling" in *Winds of Change: A Colloquium in Music Education* (New York: American Council for the-Arts and the University of Maryland at College Park, 1993), p. 31.

16. Paul Lehman, "Music in Today's Schools: Rationale and Commentary," (Reston, VA: Music Educators National Conference, 1987), 7 and 8.

17. See Charles Fowler, "Redefining the Mission of Music Education: Teaching the Value of Music," a speech delivered at the University of Maryland's Symposium: Winds of Change, April 1993 (New York: American Council for the Arts and the University of Maryland at College Park, 1993).

Composer Morton Subotnick provides insight into his own work in multimedia arts, technology in music, and composition processes through demonstration and commentary about his compositions and his computer-assisted composition program for children.

The Music and Musicians of the Future

By Morton Subotnick

I was interested in what Charles Fowler said in his talk, especially the problem that we all face as composers, musicians, and people involved in the arts in general, but especially in music. The problem is that it's very hard for us to define what music is about. Sartre said, "Music doesn't mean anything, but it's meaningful." One of the reasons we have difficulty trying to establish the importance of music in schools is that we have no language outside of music to describe music. I can describe the affect of music, but I'm not going to be able to tell you about the music itself because the music has to speak to really tell you about the music itself.

I *think* one of the reasons that we cannot talk about music is—I hesitate because I'm going to tell you something as if it's true—music is a preverbal language. I think music is a basic language of communication or it represents one aspect of a basic language of communication that probably started with utterances. What kinds of utterances? Everything from "Ouch!" or "Oh"—things that express exactly what you

Morton Subotnick is a composer and head of the composition program at the Center for Experiments in Art Information and Technology at the California Institute of Arts.

feel and mean to another person exactly at that moment. Sartre said in the same essay, "Music is like a mute who reaches and touches you and a tear comes to his eye." You know exactly what's going on in that tender moment, but if someone asked you to explain it, it would probably take you a novel, and you'd never really describe it to your satisfaction. I think music is at the root of all kinds of communication that deal with the preverbal level. If we have to address preverbal things at the verbal level in order to communicate what their importance is, we have a great deal of trouble.

A second generality is that music has required, traditionally, three people: the creator or the composer, the performer, and the audience. It's impossible to imagine music that doesn't have those three elements. In painting, which is personified by what we call studio art, the painter is in fact also the performer and the audience. When a painting goes out, that is, the painter has actually seen the painting as you're going to see it—at least the object is the same, although the painter may "see" it differently because of psychology and emotions.

But in music, we have three kinds of translation. We have the composer who creates the music, we have the performer who brings it out with his own interpretation, and then the audience who hears the music. I played with the San

Francisco Symphony and toured as a performing artist up until 1964. What intrigued me about the new medium of technology, which started basically in the 1950s, was the possibility of a true studio-art medium where the composer can work on a piece of music and be the composer *and* the performer *and* the audience in the studio. So when the object goes out, in this case a recording of a composition, it is in fact the same thing that the composer had in the studio.

I'd like you to understand that when I first began talking about the composer as also performer and audience in the early 1960s (and it wasn't just me saying this, there were a few others too), my colleagues, at that time symphony orchestra players, literally would not talk to me at times because they thought that what I was saying meant the end of performance as we know it: that is, the performing of musical instruments. That is not the case at all.

After all, the piano can play all the notes. You can play everything on the piano. With two pianos you can play all the symphonies of Beethoven and this in no way has done anything to diminish the performance of Beethoven's symphonies by orchestras. Music that has been conceived for a particular medium needs to be written for that medium. Once it is for that medium, it brings us new ways of thinking and new ways of experiencing. How could people in the Baroque period, even if they had wanted to, think of the kind of music that Liszt was writing? The grand piano of Liszt's generation required a particular kind of music, and it caused people to begin to think differently and feel differently. They had *new* thoughts and *new* feelings that they could not have had before.

We've known this from the beginning of the first cities. In these cities, there were people who made their living not by producing food and other goods, but by actually selling things to people who were passing through. Once these cities came into being, new ideas were brought from one place to another. New ideas meant that people could think in new ways. New ideas and new thinking sometimes destroy some of the old, but more often, we hope they add to the full possibility of being human.

What we are trying to do in the establishment of new media and new tools is to fulfill more of the potential of the human being. We have no idea what that potential is. I think we just need to keep working at it. As educators, and for me as a composer, it's part of what we need to do.

So when I say that the composer could become the three people—composer, performer, audience—I don't mean that now the composer won't be writing for string quartets. But what we need to begin to think of is the recording medium as an entity unto itself in which new art, new thought, and new feelings can come into play.

My final general comment has to do with the language of music, which I will talk about more tomorrow when I talk about the children's program. The children's program is designed at the level of finger painting. I'll just briefly tell you about that because it's apropos to what I'm about to say.

When a three- or four-year-old child begins to finger paint, he or she does so without thinking about imitating anything. He or she is not trying to do anything—it's part of the body. And visual artists feel this way—that the brush is part of the body and they make designs. I remember when my daughter was about four years old and doing this kind of painting. She was using brushes and all sorts of stuff. I said to her, "Gee, that's really nice." And she said, "Oh, but it's not finished." So I said, "What do you mean it's not finished?" She said, "Well, there's going to be a big yellow thing down here." She had planned this page. I said, "So, what is it?" and she said. "It's just a design, Dad." She was into modern art without realizing it. I think kids tend to have a sense of design as a joy of dealing with art.

Now think about what we have in music. There's no equivalent. We can hit sticks and we can pound at the piano, but we actually can't make music shapes and things with music until we have some technique. So what happens is that students go to the piano and learn technique. How do they learn technique? They learn scales. Well, not all musical languages have scales. By the time they have gotten enough technique to improvise and compose, it would be as if you said to them, "You cannot finger paint, you've got to draw people. You've got to draw perspective. That's the first thing you've got to learn to draw before you can attach anything to the page." Anyway, I'll get into that tomorrow and show you a program that allows the equivalent of fingerpainting in music.

The language of music has reflected, as most thinking has reflected, basic metaphors of thinking throughout history. When you think (and we have to do this quickly because this in itself is a whole lecture or two) of the eighteenth century, the basic metaphor in Western culture was the Newtonian world of weights, of balances, and of reactions. If you look at the music at the time, it began to develop into the question–answer rhetoric, almost like language itself. Our language. And it felt good and it worked very well. That tonality and that particular language was accepted and used. It was a common language.

The nineteenth century comes along and the metaphor shifts, and the main shift was to evolution. In the era of Newtonian physics, everything was in place, a kind of perpetual motion. Evolution comes along and says things aren't perfect. Things are in a state of flux; they are changing, and most people thought of them as moving in a direction—evolving in a direction. What music do you have in the nineteenth century? The epitome of it is Wagner, who evolves and evolves and never settles anywhere. It's just always going. You have Beethoven's Ninth Symphony. The big problem is how do you get rid of the double bar in the middle with the repeat sign? Think of the "Ode to Joy." How do you go back to the beginning again? We've just made it all the way to heaven and now you can't go back because the idea was to move in a direction.

The problem we've had in the twentieth century and why we are in a post-modern and not a modernist period right now is that the modernist movement was essentially relativity based.

Relativity is one of the homeliest metaphors ever. You can see it in education. All those attempts in education—it doesn't matter what you teach first, you don't have to teach history in order—are all part of the relativity metaphor.

In music, we have John Cage, who said that anything is okay in any order possible, and Arnold Schoenberg, who said we have the twelve tones where every note is absolutely equal and you can't repeat anything until you've gone through all twelve. Those were the two systems that came out of the modernist period, and they are perfect for the relativity metaphor. And it is not a metaphor you can take home easily and put in your pocket.

We are now at the threshold, at the turning point. Right now relativity is no longer, as our politics has shown us, a viable metaphor. As with Newtonian physics and as with evolution, it no longer works for us as a metaphor.

We are searching for a new metaphor, and at the same moment that we are searching, we are also developing a whole set of new tools by which we search and begin to interact with each other. Whatever we do with telecommunications and technology and all those things is going to coincide with whatever metaphor it is that we're dealing with right now, just like the Constitution of the United States happened at the moment Newtonian physics was at its prime. I don't know what the new metaphor is, and I don't think that the people who made the Constitution knew they were dealing with Newtonian physics. But we can see now that they were. So we have to be very careful because whatever we are doing is going to be in place for a long time.

The medium I'm going to present is CD-ROM. Is there anyone here who does not know what CD-ROM is? [A few hands go up.] It's amazing, because two years ago there would have been a lot of hands in this audience. CD-ROM is a music publishing medium—a tool of music publishing in every aspect. I'm going to show you one of my own compositions on CD-ROM called *All My Hummingbirds Have Alibis*. It's taken me a long time to get it finished, but it's out now. It's been listed as the first work of art actually created for the CD-ROM medium, but there will be a lot more to come.

I want to walk you through this. Here is the table of contents of this book—the CD-ROM *All My Hummingbirds Have Alibis.* The way I see CD-ROM is as a four-dimensional book. Right now in music, we Have sheet music (or the score and parts), recordings of music, books about music, and educational materials about how to actually do it. With CD-ROM you can do everything in one place. You can also turn the technology around and have an educational CD-ROM, which I'll talk about in part II of this seminar. So, I'm going to skip around.

This is me, the composer. [Demonstrates computer program.] By clicking, here, the composer is going to talk to us directly. This is like an essay or maybe a liner note on the jacket of a recording. So what you will hear is a little bit about what I have to say about this music:

> I've been working with a number of techniques, as most composers have over the years. In the twentieth century, especially the second half of the twentieth century, we have had to more or less start from scratch. In the case of Mozart, ...(Excerpt from the CD ROM, *All My Hummingbirds Have Alibis*)

What I've tried to do here is record myself talking about the music. This is intended as a one-on-one experience. You have it in your home or in the corner of your classroom, but one person at a time sees this on the screen. I wanted to put this in movie form so that instead of seeing a picture of me, you would see a movie of me actually talking to you directly. When I started this piece, the technology was there, but it was way too expensive for people to have it in their homes. Now, though, any new CD-ROM that comes out will have movies in it.

Now notice what we've got here. Up in the corner of the screen it says "Views." Under "Views" you can see "Composing in the Twentieth Century" and "The Collage Works of Max Ernst," which my composition is based on. Over here, you see the table of contents so from any point in this CD-ROM you can navigate to

anywhere you want. We're talking here about a new technology that will probably range from eighteen to twenty-five dollars per CD. Just think of publishing the score of a composition itself. If you buy a score of a major work, you're going to pay fifty to sixty dollars for the score, let alone the parts. From the CD, though, you'll be able to print out your own parts. You'll be able to print out the part of the music that you what to study. The possibilities go on and on.

Let's pick up the table of contents and go to a section called "About the Music." Here's a subsection called "Use of the Text" in which I talk about the text. Here's another section called "Treatment of the Words." Here the program takes one word, the word "rise," and shows you how these sounds are actually made. Here are two examples. I click here and we will actually hear them. [Two examples are played.]

Let's go to another section about the technology. Here's a crop of the music. This section is actually a primer on how I deal with harmonic language rhythms. It plays examples from the piece and shows you how they are broken down. I didn't have enough money to do the entire thing, but if you have enough money to add recording sessions, you can actually break the parts from the score—you can have the flute player alone and so forth. Then the listener/viewer can go in and listen to just that.

Now here's a section that allows us to ask questions. Let's ask the question, for instance, "What is MIDI?" MIDI stands for Musical Instrument Digital Interface. When I click here, the engineer who actually did the work on the CD-ROM is going to talk about it. The information on the screen is not the same information that you get from his voice. It's additional information.

> To understand what happens when we make a recording of a MIDI instrument, if I were to sit down at the MIDI keyboard and play, what the computer would actually be recording is when I press the key and how hard I press it. Sometimes it can also record other parameters, but these are the two most important ones.

(Voice of the engineer from the CD-ROM, *All My Hummingbirds Have Alibis.*)

That is truly just the beginning of what's possible here. There are many examples of interacting with the CD in this program, and in the future we will be able to do even more.

Now let's go to the piece *All My Hummingbirds Have Alibis.* The piece is actually a work that's written for concert stage, as you would find out if you went through the CD-ROM. It involves four instruments and the computer. It's the third of a trilogy called *Music for Three Imaginary Ballets,* based on Max Ernst's *Collage Books.*

All three of the works involve groups of instruments and the computer. In this case, the computer is following the performance. The computer knows where the players are in their scores. It's following them and doing its part by transforming other instruments and playing other notes. In the case of a mallet instrument, when a mallet plays, words of various sorts are heard—a female voice, a male voice, my own voice scat singing. The mallet plays and you hear words. It's all in the computer and called up on the basis of what the mallets play.

This particular piece was choreographed by the National Ballet of Canada. The dancers had learned the choreography to the recording so they knew that when a particular word appeared on the screen, they should jump up in the air and twist five times. But when the musicians got there and were playing, if the mallet player played a wrong note, the screen showed the wrong word. So it became treacherous. Well, that happens a lot now because dancers are learning to recordings and musicians are imitating recordings, rather than the recordings being a reflection of the artistic creation. That is a reversal of the whole thing.

We can start anywhere in the piece we want. Let's start in "Dance Three." Now we have the image. The image only stays there long enough to read it. Now you can listen to the music. [Excerpt is played.] This in one of the scenes of the imaginary ballet, and here was the image I

mentioned on the CD-ROM. I imagined these pictures as publicity snapshots of the ballet. You see everyone in this wild position, but if you went to the ballet you'd never see it because the picture froze that magic moment. So these were the frozen moments, and I imagined what happened before and after them and made music and a choreography that was in my head or on paper.

The mouse, as you move it, changes from one image to another. It turns to an arrow over here, and that means you can go forward or backward. There are no directions anywhere: this is an all-intuitive medium. If I click, I have a choice to go to the score, the narrative, or the images. So I'm going to start the music again. [Excerpt is played.]

When you look at the narrative, it shows what the score does in words. It's telling you what you are hearing, and it goes from measure to measure as groups and divisions change. If I go back to the score, the computer will find my place in the score. If I go to the images, it will go back to whatever image we're dealing with. So the power of this as a recording and publishing medium is enormous.

Finally, I'm going to play a group of these pieces for you. These are called, "Five Scenes for an Imaginary Ballet." These don't exist in any other form than CD-ROM. This was the beginning of trying to deal with this new medium and what it means. And what it means to me is, as I said, a four-dimensional book that deals with sound, music, words—words you hear, words you read—and images. I'd like to do a whole book of etchings, for instance, and bring them to life in a different way as if they were a ballet.

Part II

When I received the invitation to speak here I was very busy, but also very interested because I think the subject is really important. First, a little bit of background about my CD-ROM composition program for kids.

In 1961, I got a job in New York as director of music for the Lincoln Center Repertory

Theater and artist-in-residence at New York University School of the Arts. The first thing I did when I got to New York was to go to the Henry Street Settlement and offer my services for Saturdays. They brought in juvenile delinquents and underprivileged children on Saturdays. It was the very beginning of the synthesizer at that point, and I worked for almost a year with about fifteen kids from the ages of about twelve to sixteen. It was very difficult to understand why there were bars on the windows and guards at the doors because these kids were eager and interested. They were just no problem.

One of the kids was Reese Chatham. As a result of working with me through those years of junior high and high school, Chatham eventually became a composer. He's quite well known in avant-garde circles, and he lives in Paris now. He started The Kitchen, which is the main alternative space, or was, in New York.

I say this because over the years I have worked with numbers of both younger and older people in groups of ten, fifteen, or twenty. I'm convinced, if you put enough energy into it and you connect with them, it's a very complete experience. *You* know this, but a lot of people don't when I give these talks. One of those kids you are working with is going to make a big impact, and the impact of that one person is much greater than when we give lectures and concerts to thousands of people, because you can't make the same kind of connection there.

So, from the Henry Street Settlement experience, I developed this children's program. Actually, I came up with the basic notion for it in 1967–68, but it's only been in the last six years that technology has reached the point that made it possible for me to develop it. I've been working with the program over a period of years in several different places. First, I worked with a group of children in an arts-based private school called Crossroads in Los Angeles, then in a regular public school in Los Angeles, and finally in a school in one of the Los Angeles barrios where English is a second language and Spanish is the first language. We have had just incredible experiences. We have brought kids together.

One thing I felt very strongly about was that we wouldn't do any one-shot presentations in any of these schools. One of the terrible things some people do in the arts is to bring artists in, do a one-time lecture-demonstration, and then disappear. Either the kids don't connect at all or they connect and are frustrated. We didn't want to do that, so we worked with smaller groups and stayed with them over a period of at least three to four months. The experiences culminated in a public presentation of some of the kids' music.

In one case, we took all the Spanish-speaking kids to the Santa Monica Electronic Cafe and did a telecommunication with another group I had worked with in another city. They compared their music, exchanged music, and competed with music games. There was a general feeling, especially in the barrio, that it wasn't just the music they had learned; they had developed self-esteem. The kids felt they had done something important. They were capable of handling things that people had not thought they were capable of handling. This has been the case in various cities that we've worked in.

I'd like to emphasize that as a music-teaching or interactive device, I'm basing everything in the CD-ROM kids' program on a composer's viewpoint. That is a little different than what usually happens, for example, in the Orff method or in other approaches to music that are either listening based or performance based. The main difference from a composer's point of view is that we can move out of real time. Instead of staying in real time, we contemplate the music and go back. Even if we were to improvise, we would step back and listen to the music, like an artist does in the artist-studio model. The artist moves back from the canvas and says, "Hmmm, I think this needs to be a little bit to the left or this needs to be a little bit to the right." You don't just play music or improvise, you move back from the improvisation and make critical decisions about what you need to do. This element has been totally left out before because it's been impossible. I mean, you can't hire an orchestra for a kid and say, "Okay, you're going to listen and make decisions. Now, oboe, you do this." It was just not possible to do anything like that until this technology became available.

There are a couple of basic premises in the program. One is that the child creates his or her own music. It's done extremely easily in a number of ways, as you will see. Another premise is that I see the music world as a three-person model—composer-performer-listener. But the composer is also a three-person model—composer-performer-listener.

I have three CDs currently on three different levels. First, there is a finger-painting level for very young children—*Making Music*. They just get involved in it physically. Then the CD on the second level—*Making More Music*—is in non–real time, and here students have a "pencil." They can contemplate their music even before they hear it, and they can say, "Look, I'll put a note here and I'll put a note there," and so forth. The third CD—*Playing Music*—takes the pencil idea and a graph, and it turns the graph into the beginnings of notation and the staff system so that it becomes more like regular music. These CDs also offer the opportunity to alter music so they learn about variations, canon, formal ideas, and various things like that.

The role of the composer as performer and listener is very critical to me, and it's why I have divided the program so carefully in this way. The composer is the person who says, "I've got this idea." Mozart said, "I heard the entire overture to *Don Giovanni* in two minutes." Well, that's not possible because the overture to *Don Giovanni* takes longer than two minutes. So he meant something else. What he meant from the composer's standpoint, I believe (and he won't be here to dispute this), is "Ah. That's it, the overture to *Don Giovanni*." Then he wrote it in one night, all of the parts and everything.

As a composer, then, you look at what you have written, read it, and say, "No, not right. This isn't right over here." How do you know it's not right? Because there's a feedback loop that is the performer in you. When the composer reads and listens to his music, he says it is not

quite right when it doesn't match the "ah" inside. So the composer goes back and forth and questions as he's listening, "What's wrong with it? Hmm, I don't know." The performer in him says, "Let's try it a little faster, let's try it a little higher." Then the composer reads it back again and says, "Ah." Or in jazz, when someone's playing a solo and someone else says, "Yeah!" what does that mean? It means it's right. How do we know it's right? It's all matching up—composer and performer.

Now let's take a look at the composition program for kids. You see here a time canvas on the screen. Using the mouse, which moves in time, we make a design related to the melody. We can set the speed of that time and we can play it. Then we can edit in all kinds of ways. If I click on the plus sign, the notes get bigger, which is louder, or minus for smaller and softer. We can play this design backwards, upside down, or even backwards and upside down, and then back in its original form. We can make it slower; we can make it faster. We can also edit by using cut and paste.

These are all commands that are normal to the computer, so the kids are also learning computer language. I've made a copy of this music, and every time I move it you can hear the first note gets transposed. I can also take part of it, cut it, and paste it back again. I can take the bottom two notes and move them up. I can take another part and move it above itself—just any kind of combination. The editing is probably going to be used by composers because the techniques are very fast and very easy.

The basic learning principles of the entire program from beginning to end are "same" and "different." Here's the first ear-training game using the same and different principles.

> Computer: Do you want to play the game "Same or Different"?
> Subotnick: Yes.
> Computer: Here we go. [Two short melodies are played.] Was the second music the same or different?
> Subotnick: Whatever music the student has created, the computer analyzes it, knows it, and

plays with or alters it. So I'll say no, I didn't hear the difference. Then the computer will play the two tunes again. The game goes through all kinds of differences, but all kids have to do the first time is determine whether the music is same or different.

At the beginning level, there is no need to read anything. Directions are given by icons and people talking. Kids choose a square with the pictures of people in it. Each person is a guide and there is a little movie that guides them through with animation. Now here is a harder game.

> Computer: Do you want to play the game "Name That Difference?"
> Subotnick: Yes.
> Computer: Listen carefully. [Two short melodies are played. The second is slower.] Did you hear the difference? If not, press the "Listen again" button, and I'll play it for you one more time.
> Subotnick: We'll say yes, we heard the difference.
> Computer: Use the buttons to tell me how the music was different.
> Subotnick: The concepts, or possible answers are listed here. If you asked kids if the music was same or different, they might say same because they don't really think that being slower makes it different. When playing the game, they begin to get that notion for the first time.
> Computer: Congratulations. The answer "slower" is correct. Do you want to play again?
> Subotnick: Let's not. We might crash, and besides we got five points. Next there is a harder version. The harder version is when the music doesn't show up on the screen. You have to just listen. You can't see the difference, and you get more points for that.

Now I'm going to another idea. Just to show you what is happening, the program is making a set of variations based on the design or music I entered earlier. This first variation will be based on the first group of notes. That's the kids' music, and it's been varied. There will be a set of names in which kids tell what part of the piece is

played and determine whether the variation is the same or different. It goes through all kinds of the variations and gets very complicated if you take it all the way through.

In the second set of variations, the program puts a treble clef next to the music, and the kids can immediately see what they got. When making the variations, for example, the computer moves two notes over here, then asks "same or different?" Still different. Now the kids get the same number of notes in the second piece of music, so the quantity of notes in the two examples is equal. But when they are played, the kids can hear that they are not quite the same.

The kids are now able to get into the principle of similarity. The second piece of music is not entirely different. It's similar, but not the same. Now the game is "Name That Similarity." In this example, the number of notes are the same, the direction is the same, but the pitches aren't the same. The kids are not reading yet because you didn't tell them this was middle C, but if you go through this whole process they get very good at recognizing patterns. Before we give them the names of the notes or intervals, we give them scores. At a certain point they can hear their music and see it because they have been doing it in score form all along with trumpets, violins, and the whole thing. My guess is that they will be able to go to a normal score after working with this program.

There's one more step. In a few years, we will probably be able to talk to the computer. A voice will say, "Which way do you want your music?" and instead of clicking something, we'll say, "I'd like it backwards." I don't know how well that's going, but in another two or three years we will probably be able to eliminate most of the clicking.

Audience Question: Do the kids have their own disks to store their own pieces?

The program will be on CD-ROM, but kids will be able to share their pieces with other people who have the program by using floppy-disk storage. The CD-ROM contains the basic program, and when you get finished working on a piece, you can save it on a disk. The computer won't play it unless you have the application or program for it to speak to, but yes, they'll be able to save their own pieces. It is a treasure chest in which you'll be able to save your pieces and give them names. Then you can come back later and edit a previous composition.

We're moving at an incredible pace, and when it happens, when it really hits completely (and it won t be very long), it's going to be as big a revolution as recording was. With video in and out you'll be able to take home movies, put them in the computer, and record them. You'll be able to put your own voice or any sound you want into your piece. You'll be able to record sound and then place it in non–real time and hear it. At the finger painting level you'll be able to sing as you go. The computer will put the whole thing in there and you'll be able to edit it right on the spot so it's not just electronic in that regard. If you play an instrument you can put the instrument in there.

Let's go to another area now. This is a gadget that's battery operated. It is a sequencer and sound module with about twenty-seven voices and a keyboard built into it. I use it on airplanes. This is what we are using with the kids now, but when the program is released the sounds will all be internal to the computer.

Let me show you an example that's part of Playing My Music. In this CD-ROM program, kids are able to compose their own music, but other parts of the program move them into the role of interpretation.

By the time the students get the technique to play a piano piece like Clementi, they've been (I don't know whether it's good or bad) totally brainwashed. I've seen it with my own son. He was composing music before he started the piano. Since he's been playing piano he hasn't done much composing because he now knows what is "right and wrong." He's doing a little bit of blues now along with Beethoven, and he's really amazed at some of the chords in the music. He says, "Gee, they sound good, but are they right?"

All young piano students can play is eighteenth-century music at the beginning, and even if they do Bartok or something, it's very simple. So one of the things that I'm trying to do is to get to the interpretation process early enough that it can, conceivably, parallel technique. The idea is get at interpretation in such a way that the technique of learning the instrument is not going to take away from the interpretation.

I've used a lot of these ideas on my son. Before he started a piece, he used to look at a whole page and say, "Gosh, I have to learn all that?" Now he looks at it and says, "I actually have only four measures to learn." He can look at it and say this is same, this is the same. This is almost the same. And this is different. So I've got these two measures, and once I learn those I've got these two measures. And that's what he starts with. He learns those four measures and the rest of it just falls into place. That kind of thinking is simple, but most kids don't get it because learning the instrument is just too difficult—it's too long and hard.

Learning technique was fine when we only had one language. If we were in the eighteenth century or even the nineteenth century it wouldn't make any difference. But we're in the twentieth century, and we have not only Eurocentric music, but also lots of other kinds of music that kids are going to want to learn to play too. These languages are going to be very disruptive to technique because you have to decide what kind of technique you are doing. So the key is to get a global picture of interpretation quickly.

Audience Question: When will they be coming out with MIDI equipment that allows you to play quarter tones?

It's not the MIDI that controls pitch, it's the instrument. There are some instruments that are now being built on which you can do quarter tones and so on. I don't know whether we will include quarter tones in our first version of this program or not. It's not clear to me just yet how far we will go. But it's important. If I were doing this for three or four years, the ear-training component would have to include more than diatonic.

So the technology is there. It's not a MIDI

problem; it's a limitation of the present instruments. There are a number of instruments now where you can actually specify all kinds of tunings and create your own down to a very small interval.

Let's go back to interpretation for a moment. Last night I showed you tempo control and dynamic control. You can do a lot of interpretation with tempo and dynamic control, but now we get into something a little more sophisticated. It's rhythmic material. Most of us think of rhythm as dividing up a whole note or quarter note into subdivisions, but in fact, that's not what rhythm is from the composer's standpoint.

The first rhythm had to do with accents. The agogic accent came right from iambic pentameter and various verbal forms. Add pitch and dynamic accent and you have a basis of understanding, because that's the way language works. It's the way music works too, and it's what makes up rhythm. Rhythm is nothing but articulation—it has to do with long and short.

I gave a group of kids a keyboard, and I played the opening of a Beethoven sonata like this. [Plays by hitting keys randomly, but using the correct rhythm.] The computer has all the right notes in it, so, although they have to play the correct rhythm, the kids can't play the wrong notes. Then I said, "Now you do it." So they tried it, and at first they couldn't figure out what was going on. They couldn't figure out that they had to play the correct rhythm to make it work.

Then one kid said, "Oh. Do it again for me will you?" I did, and he immediately played it back. This kid was eleven years old and he was theoretically deprived in terms of background. He had never taken a music lesson, although he knew popular music. We were videotaping the kids, and as he played, the camera turned to the adults in the room, because no one had expected that. Everyone was sitting there—mouths open. We thought, "We've got this genius."

This boy had understood, without any discussion about quarter notes, eighth notes, or sixteenth notes, exactly what made his first interpretation wrong and the other right. Then we went to the next kid and it was the same. There was only one out of the five kids that never got it. He never quite managed; he understood, but he couldn't articulate with his hand. He could hear when the other kids got it right, though.

We've only tried this with those five kids, which is a very small sample, I admit. But it's clear to me, once you leave out all the baggage of quarter notes, eighth notes, and sixteenth notes, that the gesture is there. Kids hear it, and they can do the "Ah" thing with it. We are going to put this into the program and they'll be able to play games with it.

What's important here is this: if you've taught ear training, you just know that it's all wrong because kids don't get it—there's not enough information. It's like saying we're going to teach you grammar without any meaning. That's what we did for years and some people got it because they loved that kind of stuff. But as soon as meaning is added, we do better. We understand that now in teaching language. In music, you get all the information you need for meaning when you can hear the chord. Why? Because it's accented. It's higher and longer. Kids don't have to learn that, they just know automatically. It is the same thing in language—if they want to say "please," they make it higher and longer. They already know how language works. Every kid does. "Gimme." "No." These are agogic accents with amplitude and pitch thrown in. That's all Beethoven is. Kids hear it and know it because it's already part of their ability to communicate *and* it's in the music. That's my assessment. It's why the first boy was able to play the Beethoven. He wasn't memorizing abstract things. He understood the language of the music from the start.

In my CD-ROM program, what's going to happen—what I'm hoping will happen—is what happens in fingerpainting. My guess is that, as in fingerpainting, there's a point at which a kid says, "I like what I'm doing. I'm getting balance and this is fun, but I'd also like to represent something. I'd like to do an airplane, a boat, a flower." And as they do, they discover interpretation and technique.

My father painted, and we put some of his paintings up in my son's room when he was about five years old. One was a painting of some horses and another one was a clown. My son is Jacob Subotnick, named after my father, and on the painting it says Jacob Subotnick. My son said, "That's my name on it." I said, "Yes, that was your grandfather," and we talked a little bit about it. This was before school, about 7:00 in the morning. Jacob leaves for school at 8:00. Well, we couldn't get him out of his room. We walked in there and he was painting. He was trying to paint the horses. He said, "You know, this is not easy. I think I know what my grandfather was thinking when he did this, and it wasn't easy." He worked for two weeks, and he finally got something that looked something like the horses. He then started taking painting lessons because he wanted to learn how to do it.

And that, I think, is what we are after here. The kids start playing their music, they compare it to Beethoven or whatever, and they begin to understand meaning without talking about it. They understand agogic accent, not with the word, but with the sound. And then they discover that it's not easy. When they understand why there are techniques and what they are going to achieve at the other end, we can begin to really teach them technique. They have already achieved it with this program in some way. That's why painting in general is so far ahead—we can get to the technique so much faster. I think it's why our visual ability to be able to understand is so great. It's been around us and it's easier to do from the time we are kids.

Audience Question: Until your program is available, what would you suggest in terms of what to do with our students right now?

I used to think what kids did in kindergarten was just terrible. We'd sit around and sing songs and wouldn't get to the heart of the music. I no longer think that's true. But one of the things we weren't able to do—step back, listen again, and make changes—just couldn't be done effectively until a program like this was available.

What you might be able to do with a small group of kids is get into the process of "same and different." Take a look at musical patterns on a page. Don't worry about whether the children can actually read the music, just look at the patterns. It's like when we learn to read—it's all just crazy, then all of a sudden it pops in, and as you look you can see patterns. Teach kids that.

You can listen to patterns too. Play a tune, play a fragment, or listen to a fragment. Make it a game—same or different. You can do that easily. You don't have to have a computer to get at patterns from a listening standpoint.

From a composing standpoint, I think you can get at some generalities. For instance, if you play piano, you could play a piece and have the children interpret it. Play it faster, play it slower, play it louder, accent these notes now, and so on. Allow them to say, "Let's try it that way" and begin to hear what happens when you change the loudness, the speed, or particular notes. Let them actually interpret music right from the beginning.

If you have a MIDI setup, you're in good shape because you can do a lot of interpretation with some programs. It's hard, but you can do it. You can't do the algorithms, where kids play their pieces into the computer and change them immediately. You can have them make a piece and do all listening, though. You'd have to make any necessary changes for them or help them to make changes, and you can't do it on the fly. But with current programs, you can play an existing piece backwards and so on, and do it immediately. Some of those things are available now, such as changing tempo and amplitude, and associating single notes, especially if the students are older.

Audience Question: I believe in what you are doing, but I am also concerned about getting this kind of technology into freshman theory classes where it is needed. When are we going to catch up in our colleges and universities?

It's hard, but I think there are two things. First, there's no reason you can't do it, and by trying you will. Second, if we can get this kind of program to kids, they'll be using it by the time they get to freshman theory anyway.

Audience Question: How can we get more information about this program?

We have been doing a lot of work with telecommunication. What we could do is to set up little labs anywhere in the country. Then, on a monthly or bimonthly basis, we could do a telecommunication of kids and teachers to talk about different things. It would be great for us because were are in the process of programming and we need as much input as we can get. *Making Music* was published by Voyager in 1995.

Audience Question: You've given us a picture of explosion of creativity. Kids will likely have access to this program, and they will come to school having done this. How will our future programs have to change to cope with this?

We're going to be forced into major changes, no question about it. It's an extremely exciting time right now. Scary, but exciting.

Audience Question: Do you have a vision for what this culture looks like?

Yes, I have two visions. One is my vision and the other is the probable outcome. My vision is that we are going to have a much more articulate civilization worldwide. Articulate not just with words, but with the things that we are talking about—the ability to be able to cry at the right time and to laugh at the right time, because that is really what art and music are about. It's about opening the doors to that communication. Once we understand—and the "ah" principle is only one aspect—that one can communicate at this level and other levels, there will be a great opening. It is not something we ordinarily think about, but I think technology can offer the possibility of worldwide immediate communication—of understanding when a person does *that*, it's the same or different.

Audience Question: Will your program be compatible with other computers?

Yes, it will be compatible with all kinds of computers. For example, we're doing it on the 9th of October in conjunction with MTV and Nickelodeon for handicapped kids in Santa Monica and New York. We're developing ways in which handicapped kids can work with it. That's why we're getting the voice in there, so that there are various ways kids can input. They are going to be sharing their work in the two cities over the telephone line.

Sally Monsour points to both our heritage and our missions as she considers the future of general music education. While calling for a rededication to the historic mission of "music for everyone," she also focuses on the need for the profession to emerge from isolation and seek connections with school, local, and global communities. The future of general music lies in our ability to reach out to these communities and to provide meaningful music opportunities and experiences for all.

General Music Tomorrow

By Sally Monsour

As we sit here tonight, we can feel alright about the future because of what an eight-year-old boy said in a general music class when asked his opinions about music. He said, "Why, music is about the oldest thing we have around and we still have it in perfectly usable condition."

Our Mission

With that thought still lingering in your minds, I would like to begin by saying a few words about our mission—a mission that our forebears also championed over the past several decades. If they were present for this symposium, they would be cheering us on because they too were challenged by the tomorrows they confronted. They tried to adapt and develop, to advocate and defend. They gave us a mission as well as a heritage. While that mission has been extended to meet changing times, its most essential elements are the same today and will be tomorrow.

On this occasion, it would be well to rededicate ourselves to that mission. It is a mission that every general music professional knows by

heart: "Music for everyone"—a total citizenry that is taught music in a way that will improve the quality of their lives regardless of career or age, culture or social place. With such a mission, everyone is musically acknowledged, no one is overlooked; everyone is encouraged to sing without selectivity; everyone is taught to play musical instruments regardless of skill level; everyone is led to feel and express musical ideas in movement regardless of motor development; everyone is presented with opportunities to listen perceptively to all kinds of music; and everyone is a composer. These are the people we serve and invite to the musical table. In the best tradition of general music, they have always been welcome. As each tomorrow beckons, let us increase our efforts on their behalf, because this is our mission and these are our people.

Increasingly, our people will be found outside of a traditional K–12 schoolroom—in early learning centers, retirement communities, and recreation programs. Wherever they are—in the inner city or in small towns—the schools and educational programs in their communities should be alive with intergenerational learning, with the singing of songs, with dancing, with the playing of traditional instruments, and with the creating of musical pieces. Through such programs, our mission will be fulfilled because an important element will have been added to

Sally Monsour is professor of music at Georgia State University in Atlanta, Georgia.

the qualities of these people's lives.

During any one week, there are several million people of all denominations in a religious service of some kind. How many will want to participate in the congregational singing that most of these services will include? How many will do so because they were taught and enjoyed singing in a general music class sometime in their past? It is our hope that more and more will, because these are our people and their musical enjoyment and subsequent participation is our mission.

Let us look now to another kind of mission for general music, one that has to do with the ecology of music—its place as a natural part of our life-environment. This idea is captured in a true statement written by an eight-year-old in response to the question "What is music?" She wrote: "Music is all of the good things I hear. It is loud and soft and fast and slow. But I can hear music in the ticking of a clock or when my sister jumps rope, and to the woman next door who is going deaf, music is waking up in the morning and finding out that she can still hear the birds."

Perceiving the sounds around us in musical ways, as this child did, will enable us to make more sense of our environment. To be one with such a world can contribute to the joy of living. While this is not a new concept by any means, it needs to be emphasized at this critical time, for as I see it, the floodtide of educational change could cause us to lose our way and deter us from this important mission.

Making Connections

Given predictions of tomorrow's educational climate, what can we do to assure that general music programs will be valued, maintained, and expanded? One thing is certain, we will have to join together with other educators within the school as well as with people outside in the community. We will need to see ourselves as part of a whole, to actively reach out to all relevant groups. We should overtly demonstrate the expectations that we have in common with all educators and increase efforts to broadcast the goals we share with other school subjects.

Within the school itself, general music teachers should make stronger connections with all other teachers and administrators including teachers of the other arts and of performance classes and ensembles. While many systems have already established such relationships, the full-hearted support by all music and arts educators toward shared educational goals is too long overdue.

Reaching beyond the bricks and mortar of school buildings and connecting the school with the home is another positive step toward making music a part of living. Educators have long felt that the home should become an extension of what is learned in school, and with predictions of future technology, this could become possible in ways we would not have dreamed of in the past. Interactive technology is presenting opportunities for family music making and composing. Students can bring their music into the school to be shared with peers. Will we be ready to receive their efforts? Will we understand the process that went into their work? Will we return to the home creative music projects from our classes? As a result of user-friendly music-making instruments, new levels of communication will be forthcoming. Many people have wanted to create the music we "heard" within ourselves, but then there was the notation to master or the instrument to learn. Now our ability to express feelings and ideas in musical and artistic ways could become a reality for people of all ages.

Another way to look at connections is to make sure that parents and community leaders are supportive of our goals, especially those that they perceive as valuable in the emerging new age—an age that for many will be fraught with single parenting, job loss or dislocation, and economic hardships of all kinds. We will need to make clear our concern for building self-esteem and the feeling of belonging, as well as the ability to cope with change by giving learners practice in creative problem solving. Music experiences are well-suited to accomplish such goals in ways we all know so well. By doing so, we will not have to give up musical priorities in either content or method. We can do it all if we focus on connecting with others and breaking out of our isolation. Another important part of this community are the professional musicians, including private teachers, who should be drawn into our instructional programs. Despite the well-intentioned and sometimes successful efforts to use community talents within the school, the surface has barely been scratched when compared to the positive benefits of true collaboration.

Connections that cause educational programs to become more inclusive can also be seen in contemporary concepts of school restructuring. Model programs are taking root in communities that have learning centers with flexible schedules, the combining of grade levels, parent and teacher choice, and new methods of assessment. Such centers will house not only traditional subject-centered classes, but also an almost unbelievable array of courses, social services, and learning opportunities for all ages. Reform of this type may not typify every school system, but it is predicted that elements will filter into all educational programs. And as general music educators, we must not miss such a circle of musical opportunity—one that has the force and vitality to make the vision of lifelong music learning a reality at last.

We will also experience connections that are increasingly global. Tomorrow's general music educators will reminisce as they look back on the time before visual/aural linkups such as electronic field trips to a Cajun folk festival or the Vienna Opera, or musical performances, demonstrations, and student electronic interchanges between Savannah and Singapore or Chicago and Brazil.

When thinking about the necessity of greater unity and less fragmentation, a statement made by William Lepley, director of the Iowa Department of Education, seems very appropriate: "We must not tear down a system that has served so well, but we must have an educational barn raising, where we all come together as partners, bringing together our collective commit-ment, cooperation, and hard work to create an educational system for 2010 that gives us reason to celebrate and be festive because we created it together" (p. 156).

Building toward Success

There are things we have come to know, or at least reasonably suspect, about being successful in the teaching of general music. We have learned them by experience, by observation, and through research. For our teachers of tomorrow, we need to unleash these "truisms" by every means at our disposal. We know very well, that our ideas may change, and we will adjust accordingly, but what is needed right away is our best effort toward building successful programs.

Beginning immediately, the slogan "Teach for Success" should be our hallmark. What are some of the ideas that could point us in this direction? Here is the beginning of a list:

■ If the power and magic of music becomes accessible when we draw people into the music itself, we should keep the musical sound alive throughout the lesson with active learning using interesting, quality music.

■ If musical achievement is advanced by building on the natural connections between feeling, thinking, and doing, we should work toward the totality of the musical-artistic experience—a holistic experience.

■ If problem solving is basic to the full development of our human capacity, we should plan lessons in which learners discover and create.

■ If effective lessons emerge from what goes into a lesson plan and not from the plan itself, we should learn to trust our own creative abilities, involve students in our planning, and use the language of possibilities.

■ If people have distinctive musical voices that contain memories, feelings, and traditions, we should use these to ensure that diversity is appreciated and that ethnic doors open for both going in and coming out.

■ If learners experience difficulty in focusing attention, we should keep them motivated by using variety, personalization, and relevance—

always challenging them toward their highest potential.

■ If our programs are often too complex, too jam-packed, or overburdened with details, we should simplify and do well that which we undertake, focusing our attention on the possible and the teachable.

■ If promising more than we can successfully accomplish leads to disappointment and frustration, we should verify the substance of our programs, avoiding confusing verbiage and inaccurate appraisals of achievement.

Of course, each person here could add more to such a list, but whatever list one uses, it should stress what will be successful. It should drive out failure and cause mediocrity to fall away. As it is now, there are too many unsuccessful programs, too much skill building without enjoyment and meaning, and too many teachers without enthusiasm for the mission of general music. We must face up to our inadequacies. It would be tempting to reason them away, but doing so will leave us with too many wasted yesterdays.

Positive Change

And now what about change itself, positive change? It is clear that educational reform is in a forward momentum and that in many places general music programs are keeping up. There is a deep concern and commitment, a sense of direction and action. People involved in such programs are rejecting isolation and the failed programs of the past. The protective barriers of one teaching method over another are coming down, and differences are being respected for what can be learned rather than guarded. And what is more, the new leadership in our ranks has the necessary vision and, more important, the will to confront our uncertain, but exciting future.

Not all innovations have been successful and, as we move forward, we will naturally be confronted with plateaus. Most of all, we will need to learn *how* to change, for change is never easy or automatic, even given commitment. Different

options will be available to us, and during this symposium, we have been given the opportunity to consider some of them. One thing is sure: the options we choose should be made in light of clear goals and not for purposes of innovation alone or change for the sake of change. Let us free ourselves and our teachers from the bandwagon mentality. Let us change with rational underpinnings.

I feel optimistic about general music tomorrow for many reasons. There is the research taking place in cognitive psychology that gives us a comprehensive view of human development—one that considers the wide range of human capabilities, talents, and yes, the very nature of what it means to be intelligent. This work should enable us to better assist learners in such areas as aural perception and sensory integration.

Yes, we are witnessing an upswing, a new vitality in our educational establishment from early learning centers through adult education. Credit for these advances goes to educational leaders, parents, and the public at large, but also to professional associations, such as the Music Educators National Conference, that are initiating advocacy groups and coalitions. They are exerting their influence in new and important ways. Suffice it to say that were it not for MENC and the Society for General Music, we would not have gathered for this symposium.

Another reason for a positive attitude toward the future comes out of the vision statement for arts education in the *National Standards for Arts Education* (published by MENC in 1994). The statement is a beautifully worded call for the arts in the many ways they can be essential.

Finally, when addressing the topic of general music tomorrow, I would lean heavily toward a tomorrow that will say to everyone who will benefit from our instructional programs, "We will work harder to make our mission a reality. It makes no difference where you are from, how you learn, or what talents you possess, we will find a secure and appropriate place for you in general music."

And now, I would like to close with a true

story. Not long ago, in our field-based methods course in an inner-city school, a preservice student and myself were stopped by a fifth-grade boy who wanted to show us the crystal ball he was holding. He asked us to look into it and, of course, we saw nothing. We asked what he was seeing in his ball. He said: "I see my class singing, but not me. I don't know how to sing." As we gathered our thoughts for a reply, he pointed to his new music teacher and said: "Will you teach me?" And with that question and all that it implies, I would like to close by saying to all of us here and to the many general music educators everywhere, "Let's *teach* the world to sing!"

Reference

Lepley, W. 1991. "Iowa in the year 2010" in Cetron, Marion and Margaret Gayle, *Educational renaissance: our schools at the turn of the twenty-first century*. New York: St. Martin's Press.

Section 2

Issues for Tomorrow's General Music Programs

No reconceptualization of the role of music education in tomorrow's schools would be valid without considering issues currently at the forefront of educational debate. Political and economic concerns, as well as cultural and social changes, fuel the momentum of the reform movement. Ideas and issues raised extend to and must be considered by educators in every curricular subject, including music.

The authors of articles in this section, all speakers for special topics sessions at the symposium, represent diverse perspectives in music education—from practitioner to researcher, from teacher to administrator, from public school educator to university faculty. The issues they address are equally diverse. Assessment in general music is considered by Scott Shuler and Jennifer Davidson. Marvelene Moore and Ellen McCullough-Brabson share thoughts about music and cultural diversity. Additional reflections on teaching in a musically diverse world are provided by Will Schmid. Peter Webster and Jacqueline Wiggins write about creativity and the place of technology in the future of music education, and Daniel LeJeune discusses technology in the future of music education. Carol Scott-Kassner and coauthors Plato Karafelis and Rob Hugh provide insight about integrating music instruction with other areas of the school curriculum.

Scott C. Shuler summarizes past and current thinking on assessment in general and evaluation in the arts in particular. While the arts lead the education community in some aspects of assessment, he notes, we neglect or entirely exclude some dimensions of music instruction and learning from meaningful evaluation. Shuler challenges music educators to reexamine curricular goals and the purpose of testing as we revise current evaluation tools and build new means of assessing what students know and can do in music.

Assessment in General Music
Trends and Innovations in Local, State, and National Assessment

by Scott C. Shuler

The purpose of this article is to outline general trends and innovative developments in assessment at the local, state, and national levels. Generalizing about trends in a field as diverse as music education is difficult; the profession is not like a river, in which all the water flows in the same direction. Our field is, rather, like an ocean, where the tide is often going in and out at the same time, depending on which coast we are observing. For example, local districts in some states are hiring new music teachers, while others are laying them off. To generalize is always dangerous.

In this article, I'll provide a brief overview of assessment in the field of education and how music education has followed—or occasionally led—that field. Then I'll discuss trends in arts assessment at the state level. In the process, I'll describe the State Collaborative on Assessment and Student Standards (SCASS) arts assessment project, of which I am cochair. Next, I'll discuss plans for the 1997 National Assessment of

Scott C. Shuler is music consultant for the Connecticut State Department of Education in Hartford, Connecticut.

Educational Progress (NAEP) in the Arts, with which I have also been involved in various capacities. Finally, I'll speculate about what the future of classroom music assessment might be like.

Music assessment is essential. Although many schools struggle to maintain their ideals, public pressures typically force them to set curriculum priorities as follows:

1. What is tested.
2. What is mandated.
3. What is best for children.

Currently music qualifies under number 3 or, if we're lucky, our state has a mandate for music instruction that places us at level 2. Until we reach priority level 1, however, our position will not be secure, because we will not be able to demonstrate the difference that we make for students and the inequities that exist between districts in the opportunities to learn music. Assessment will not be a panacea for all of our problems, but good assessment will certainly help.

Background on Assessment in Music

Historically, teachers of music and the other arts have been rather insecure, maybe even a little schizophrenic, about assessment. For years, some of us thought that the arts were behind the rest of the educational world because we didn't have enough scantron tests—the tests that require #2 pencils and have lots of little bubbles to fill in. At that point in history, as now, our objective was to achieve credibility with the rest of the field of education. We apologized for our lack of tests, while some of our finest minds developed measures such as the *Music Achievement Test* (Colwell)[1] and the *Musical Aptitude Profile* and *Iowa Test of Music Literacy* (both by Gordon).[2] Our profession was busy doing what we thought good educators should do.

Other music educators said, "If that's assessment, then forget it," and turned their backs on assessment in general. They said, "Assessment seems to be something that you do with a #2 pencil, and that's not what music education is all about. Therefore, we're not going to *do* assessment." They noticed there was only one standardized measure that dealt with music performance, the *Watkins-Farnum Performance Scale,*[3] and that was nothing to write home about. They concluded that no appropriate means of assessing performance existed and that standardized tests were trivial and inappropriate for the arts.

Ironically, while music test developers and test skeptics argued, many music educators were busy conducting assessment. We were doing assessment every time we had an adjudicated music festival. Every time we decided who we were going to allow to enroll in a music school, we were assessing. We would "roll our own" combination of criteria—such as intonation and tone quality—to screen potential students. We were focusing almost exclusively on music performance and we were inconsistent in our criteria for evaluation, but we were assessing. Our profession's challenge today is to build on the assessments that we have always been doing well, and try to address some of the important content areas that we have neglected.

Standardized Tests and Assessment Technology

One of the problems with standardized tests

is curriculum alignment. A test purchased off the shelf assesses whatever that test is designed to measure. A commercial test probably doesn't measure the content of your curriculum guide or what you want students to learn in your district. Another problem with standardized tests is that they tend to *trivialize* content. In other words, the content measured by the test is usually not what we care about the most, but merely what we can assess on a scantron sheet with a #2 pencil.

Better assessment technologies can help us "stretch the envelope" and assess areas that were previously difficult or impossible to examine. In the early twentieth century, students took pencil-and-paper tests that asked them to match Italian terms (allegro, rubato, etc.) with their definitions. Later, phonographs enabled us to include recordings of music in tests. The invention of cassette tapes carried us a step farther by allowing us to record and evaluate student performances. Now, digital sound technology may be preparing us for yet another evolutionary step. Synthesizers and other MIDI equipment provide students with powerful opportunities to compose music.

Not that we haven't been creative with older technology. In our effort to develop standardized tests, some very noble attempts can be found. In the Silver Burdett tests developed for one of the older editions of that textbook series, Richard Colwell designed some very creative pencil-and-paper solutions for assessing musical knowledge of children who couldn't read very well, particularly in the early grades.[4] The tests captured some of the important content of that series; however, they didn't get at many of the things that we care about most, for example performance.

The Good Test

What is appropriate assessment? I agree with Grant Wiggins, who says that we should design tests that are so *authentic,* that so accurately address what we really care about, that when we "teach to the test" we are providing good instruction. If your program is driven by a test, it had better be a *good* test, because if you are driven by a *bad* one, you are in deep trouble. When we provide evidence of results to the people who hold us accountable—school boards, legislators, administrators, communities—and they look at test scores, we have put all our eggs in that basket.

I'll give you an example in music. How many elementary teachers do you know who feel their entire curriculum is oriented toward the winter concert? Why? Because the concert is the only yardstick the community has to measure the success of the music program. One can argue, "If that's what the community expects, we have to give it to them." The fact is that if the concert is all members of the community see, that is how they will judge the music program. The system perpetuates itself in a vicious cycle.

Is it possible to create assessment measures that deal with what we really care about? If yes, then we could orient the curriculum toward the assessment, teaching to the test, without sacrificing our integrity. On the contrary, we could improve our credibility with the public while improving our programs. We must be certain, however, that our assessments are authentic; that is, that they capture the essence of what children should be learning and omit nothing important.

Arts Educators as Assessment Innovators

A few years ago I had a chance to chat with Lee Shulman, a professor at Stanford University. One of his projects is developing teacher assessment centers in which young teachers are monitored by their peers. In a music teacher assessment center, for example, a group of experienced music teachers might ask a novice teacher questions about teaching music reading or even watch that teacher implement a lesson with students.

As we talked about teacher evaluation, Shulman commented on how well musicians evaluate performance. He said, "You know, what I'm really looking for is something like a band festival. That is where you really find out

what teachers can do. We need rating sheets with clear criteria (the teaching equivalent of intonation, expressiveness, etc.) and judges who can watch and evaluate a person based on those characteristics. Ideally, the judges will be trained until they are clear on the criteria, so that if the same person performs for two different judges, each judge will award a similar rating (In assessment lingo, the scores will be "reliable"). I really like what music people are doing right now by measuring a holistic final product."

"Portfolio assessment" is a term one hears in discussions about innovative assessment approaches. Portfolios are collections of student work, usually assembled over an extended period of time (a year or more). Language arts teachers are particularly enamored of this approach. Once again, the arts led the way. Visual artists and art educators have been building and evaluating portfolios for years.

The key to building good portfolios is to make sure that they collect student work that you really care about and that you have developed clear criteria for evaluating the work that goes into the portfolio. Ideally, you should also develop a means of using the portfolio to compare the student's work over time, so you can evaluate his or her progress. Otherwise, the portfolio can become a mindless collection of everything and of little value to anyone.

There are exciting developments in technology that promise to make portfolio development and assessment more feasible. In the arts, we have been using audio- or videotapes to collect certain types of student products. Unfortunately, these media are not very compact and do not provide "random access," meaning that we often have to fast forward or reverse through a great deal of material to view or listen to a particular student or project. Computer and digital technologies are solving those problems. For example, digital cameras and video cards enable teachers to take high-quality still and moving images and store them directly onto computer disks. Teachers and students can create multimedia portfolios of student work—including art works, musical compositions, and performances—directly on disk, and can access each student file instantly. Large-capacity disk storage systems permit easy access to multimedia portfolios for all students.

Unfortunately, there are many aspects of music achievement that are rarely, if ever, assessed. Improvisation, for example, is an area in which we very rarely assess. In fact, we are still rather vague on whether or how to assess *anything* creative. If English teachers took the same approach, no one would ever write a paper. We cannot lay claim to creativity as part of our professional "territory" without assessing students' creative work. We must develop criteria for assessing original products created by students.

Trends in State Arts Assessment

There are several trends in arts assessment at the state level. The first is simply that states are seriously considering arts assessment, generally for the first time. What districts, legislators, school boards, and business people expect is evidence of student outcomes, for they have been conditioned by the media, whether rightly or wrongly, to believe that schools currently fail to educate children.

Current interest in assessment is part of the second cycle of the movement toward "account-ability" in education. Some of us remember the first cycle from the 1960s, when we learned to write behavioral objectives. In the current cycle, however, the movement is being called "out-come-based education," *except* in states where conservative constituencies such as the religious right have objected to that term. In those states, authorities choose to give the accountability movement a more complicated name, such as "setting high standards" or "defining what students should know, be able to do, and be disposed to do."

We are moving toward a system that focuses on how schools perform and how well we do in terms of helping kids to learn. Many business people and other community members don't want hear about minutes of instruction per week, numbers of computers in the school, and other "opportunity-to-learn" issues. They point out that what is *really* important is how much students are learning. Education is perceived as an accounting sheet on which learning is quantified and tallied. The good news is that, unlike the 1960s, the arts are being included in discussions of what should appear at that bottom line.

The second trend in state arts assessment is the trend toward "authentic performance assessment." "Authenticity" has to do with whether what is measured is what we care most about. As we develop authentic assessment we ask questions such as, "Is this task something that is important for kids to learn? Is this an important behavior in terms of what kids need to do for the rest of their lives?" If the answers to these two questions are "yes," we have an authentic assessment.

Another way to look at the authenticity of an assessment task is to consider whether students would ever need to perform the task in the "real world" outside the school. For example, few adults take music dictation, writing down in music notation what they hear, as part of their daily lives. Some pick up tunes by ear and a few jazz students write down improvisations by professionals, but few take dictation. If the purpose of a test is to determine whether students can write music notation, a more authentic task would be to have students notate a composition of their own creation. The latter task is authentic because, I believe, in the future a large percentage of our population will use electronic technologies to compose their own music.

"Performance assessment" involves students actually *doing* something, rather than just writing or theorizing about it. In performance assessment, students complete some kind of hands-on task, usually other than pencil-and-paper, that results in an exhibition of their learning. Performance assessment involves students in demonstrating their learning by applying it, rather than simply talking about it.

"Authentic" and "performance" assessment overlap, but are not identical. Many times, although not always, what we really care about is best assessed through some kind of hands-on project, so performance assessment is authentic. The authentic approach contrasts favorably with a written midterm exam I remember vividly from junior high band. It was a pencil-and-paper test on which we had to match Italian terms with definitions. We hadn't spent any time during the semester studying definitions; instead, we had focused on learning to perform our music. The principal, however, had told our band director that he had to administer a written test each semester if he wanted to give grades in the course. An authentic approach would have been to have us demonstrate our understanding of Italian terms by preparing an unfamiliar piece of music independently and performing an appropriate interpretation. The matching test wasn't authentic because adults are, generally, not going to define Italian terms at home. What we hope they *are* going to do is play music on an instrument. In this case, an authentic assessment requires performance.

Similarities

Both 1960s Accountability and Performance-Based Assessment require outcomes that are:

- Observable
- Linked to district and departmental goals
- Shared in advance with students and community

Figure 1. The similarities of assessment now and assessment in the 1960s.

While performance assessment is certainly the authentic way to evaluate creating and performing music, there is still an appropriate place for written work. For example, to assess students' ability to evaluate a performance using musical terminology, they could write a critique of a performance to which they have listened. There is even room for multiple-choice tests when they are well designed. In fact, such measures are an efficient way of evaluating certain areas of music learning, such as the ability to identify or analyze characteristics of music. There are many areas of music learning, however, for which such simplistic testing is inappropriate.

Differences between Assessment Now and in the 1960s

If we were to compare assessment now with assessment in the 1960s we would find several similarities (see figure 1). One of those similarities is this idea of getting to the bottom line. Now, as then, we want to be able to *observe* how much the students are learning. Now, as then, the outcomes of instruction also must be connected with the general goals of our educational system. District and department goals must be connected to a curriculum that is shared with the community.

One problem with the 1960s approach was that we developed curricula with many little parts. I have reviewed curriculum documents in schools that have only thirty-six music class sessions every year but have 160 behavioral objectives for each grade level. Not only is it impossible to keep track of so many objectives, it is also impossible to teach them all in the amount of time allotted.

There are several characteristics that distinguish what we do now from what we did in the

Differences

1960s Accountability outcomes are:	Performance-Based Assessment outcomes are:
• Often fragmented or dissected	• Holistic
• Product-oriented	• Process-as well as product-oriented
• End points	• Evolutionary
• Atomistic	• Complex
• Often low-order behaviors	• Higher-order behaviors
• Simple to score/ evaluate	• Complex to score/ evaluate
• Unidimensional	• Multidimensional

Figure 2. The differences between assessment now and assessment in the 1960s.

1960s (see figure 2). One difference is that performance assessment looks for broad tasks that require students to pull together learning from various segments of the curriculum. Students demonstrate their mastery of essential bits and pieces of musical knowledge and skill by carrying out multifaceted, "organically whole," authentic tasks. By having students perform, for example, we not only find out what they know about tempo markings, but also whether they can produce a good tone and have a concept of the style period. We evaluate all of these learnings at once instead of separately testing dozens of bits of information listed in behavioral objectives in curriculum guides.

Another important difference now from the 1960s is that when we are concerned not only about product, but also about process. Even though we are "outcome-based," striving for authentic assessment forces us to go far beyond just producing an end product. One of the assets of having students create portfolios of their work, for example, is that students must get involved in choosing their best work for their portfolios. Setting up a portfolio system in the classroom empowers students by requiring them to review what they have done and decide what they like and what they don't like. Students who can make judgments about the quality of their work not only address the National Standards, but also make progress toward becoming independent learners, capable of carrying out the musical processes without our assistance.

Authentic assessments are more complex and holistic than measuring numerous isolated behavioral objectives. Now, as in the Shulman example, we ask students to assemble all of the individual skills and knowledge they have learned and apply them by completing a limited number of complex tasks. For example, instead of having one assessment that deals exclusively with rhythm and another that deals with pitch, we might ask students to carry out a task that involves both. We evaluate their performance on the task by looking at the dimension of rhythm, the dimension of pitch, and probably a few other dimensions as well, such as voice quality or expressiveness. Hence, we extract more information from each assessment. In other words, we reduce the number of trees so that we can see the forest.

This approach is also powerful because it emphasizes higher order behaviors. When we ask students to clap rhythm patterns, we're dealing with a behavior that is not very high-order and definitely not the endgame. Few adults spend much time clapping rhythm patterns. What we *really* value is an adult who has internalized the beat, who can read and understand music that includes complex rhythms, who can maintain a steady beat and read rhythms when performing, and who feels an internal sense of movement when listening to music. The adult should also recognize when rhythm is good or not good in a performance and be able to make a value judgment about it. These are higher-order musical behaviors than clapping patterns. Along the same lines, if I were having students compose, I would be more concerned with whether they could produce a composition than with whether they could notate key signatures correctly. While we still need to create opportunities in the classroom setting to teach and monitor students' progress on individual skills and bits of knowledge, our summary assessments should reflect our ultimate goal of having students "put it all together." District, state, and national assessments should—to the extent possible—measure global behaviors.

Scoring holistic authentic tasks is more difficult than scoring bubble sheet tests. When evaluating holistic behaviors, judges must share clear "standards." To judge improvisations, for example, districts need not just one, but a faculty full of teachers who have reached some agreement about what it means to improvise at the level of expectation established in the district's curriculum guide. There must also be agreement on the dimensions, or criteria, for evaluating the students' work. Are teachers going to be listening for whether students match the harmonic accompaniment? Does a student's improvisation have to fit a certain style? Should there be a shape to the improvisation, a sense of going somewhere and then returning? Everyone must either agree on the criteria or bow to the will of the group, or there's no point in assessing. If everyone's ruler is a different length, measurement is meaningless.

For example, suppose "easy" Teacher A administers an assessment and his students all score ninety-five or above. Across town Teacher B, who has very high standards, tests her students and gives them an average score of 70. Teacher B's students may actually perform better than Teacher A's, but because the teachers' evaluation standards are different, the results

seem to indicate the opposite. This not only defeats the purpose of the assessment, but can actually cause damage to programs. When the district looks at the results of the assessment, an uninformed administrator might be tempted to label Teacher A a hero and prescribe remedial help for Teacher B.

Standards are powerful and important. What this implies is that one of the most important roles of in-service for teachers is to set standards, agree on standards, try to apply them consistently, and get together from time to time to reevaluate them. This also has enormous implications for our profession, because having National Standards requires teachers across the country to share a common vision of what quality work sounds and looks like.

Finally, as I mentioned earlier, performance assessment is really multidimensional, unlike the more unidimensional tests associated with 1960s behavioral objectives. When you deal with an authentic behavior, you tend to be looking at many dimensions at once. If you test in alignment with a behavioral objective that requires students to clap rhythm patterns in $\frac{2}{4}$, all you care about is that one dimension of rhythm. If, however, you have them sing a song that involves the same rhythms, you can assess more than the students' rhythmic accuracy. You can evaluate other dimensions of musical learning, such as tone quality and pitch.

Changing the Curriculum Paradigm

Standards and authentic assessment can help us move away from the typical curriculum model that is driven by traditional expectations (see figure 3). In this traditional model, we start by accepting the fact that we have to present Christmas/holiday/winter programs in elementary schools, produce refrigerator art, and produce the annual musical. We filter those time-honored expectations through what the district board and administrators think is important, sometimes with booster club support, until we end up with some resources. The resources and teacher interests then dictate what our program

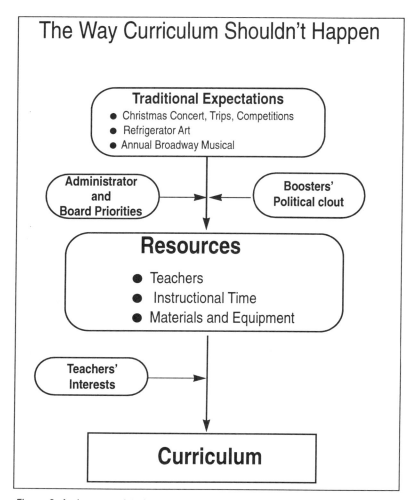

Figure 3. *An inappropriate but common curriculum model.*

is. That's the way things have traditionally happened in schools, and not just in music, or even just in the arts.

The standards movement is in part about moving away from that tradition. We're moving in the direction of saying "all right, what do the kids *need* to learn?" In this more appropriate curriculum model (see figure 4), we start by looking at existing state and national standards describing what students should learn and compare these to our local priorities and needs, in part based on assessments of what students are currently learning. We then ask, "What can our teachers do? What are the teachers' areas of expertise?" and "What are the students interest-

ed in doing?"

The issue of what interests students is important. One of the differences between the typical music program and the typical visual arts program is that music tends to offer one-size-fits-all high school curricula. By offering very little except performing ensemble classes, we say to students, "If you don't like being in groups, forget it. We don't have anything for you. There's no place for you in our program." When we do offer a classroom music course, we usually offer music theory, which is highly specialized. Such courses take students who are already in ensembles, peel off those who are particularly serious about music, and provide them with greater depth.

We should take a lesson from our colleagues in the visual arts. They have moved toward offering semester courses that interest and therefore attract a variety of students. Students can drop in for a semester, work hard, and then return a few semesters later when they have a space in their schedule. While they are in an art class, they are usually working on projects of their own design that are personal expressions and therefore important to them as individuals. Numerous types of music classes could have the same kind of appeal, such as music composition, keyboard, and guitar courses. We need to cultivate sequential semester courses in these areas to provide students with alternative paths to adult involvement with music.

We hope our new National Standards will help us move toward a broader approach. In the new, Standards-driven approach, we will base curricula on what students need to learn, customizing them to match teachers' particular areas of expertise with students' areas of interest. If we determine that kids are interested in keyboards and that they can learn what they need to know by playing them, then we had better learn to teach the keyboard. In this sense, kids determine both the curriculum and teacher in-service. Resources are provided based on what the curriculum requires. Assessment is based on the curriculum. Professional development is based on the curriculum. Professional development makes teachers better, and that in turn leads to a better curriculum.

This is a student-centered, student-driven model, and it is one of the significant contributions of the National Standards. Traditionally, when we have developed assessment, the most difficult and time-consuming process has been identifying desired outcomes. We put so much energy into identifying what students should learn that we have had little left over to design other important aspects of curriculum, including appropriate instruction and assessment. The Standards can liberate us from the preliminaries and let us get right to the heart of designing a program. Basing our curriculum on a set of national standards also gives us more credibility.

We should not become intellectually lazy, however, and just lean on the Standards uncritically. We should try to improve the Standards. Ultimately, however, the test of whether the Standards are useful is whether they allow us to focus on how we can best help our students master them (teaching strategies), and how we can find out whether we have succeeded (assessment).

We must set up a complete learning system. First, as in the Standards, we must communicate what all students should learn in our district, at the state level, and at the national level. We must create tasks, exercises, or projects that students

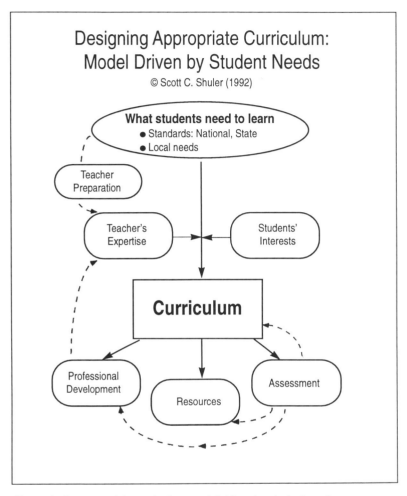

Figure 4. An appropriate curriculum model driven by student needs.

are expected to complete as evidence that they have learned. We must create in-service for teachers based on the Standards, we must conduct assessment, we must collect and examine the results, and, when we fall short, we must ask ourselves, "What do we have to do differently now? Were our curriculum standards unrealistic, or do we just need to teach better?" Then we must make the appropriate changes. That is the learning system music educators must adopt.

Questions When Designing Assessment

There are several important questions that must be answered when developing large-scale (state or national) assessments. Some of these are questions that our profession had to answer when developing our National Standards.

Do we develop our assessment (or our standards) based on what is *or what* should be? Developing assessment requires establishing expectations about what students should be able to do and then developing tasks and scoring systems to find out whether students are indeed able to do those things. Many teachers are worried about the new Standards, or about the idea of state or national assessment, because they fear they'll be held accountable for teaching skills and content they haven't the time or resources to teach. Do we base our Standards on what we think students are already learning or on what we really want students to learn? Is the test evolutionary or revolutionary?

If we want to drive instruction forward we need standards and assessment that are somewhat visionary. If we based the National Standards and assessment on what typically happens in a music classroom, neither would include much composition or improvisation. There are three approaches to developing assessment, each of which results in a different kind of test. The choice of approach is therefore one that has to be made.

First, if we believe that the purpose of testing is to prove that we are successful, then we write an assessment that makes us look good (such as a test of whether students can sing "Hot Cross Buns" with a steady beat). We then declare ourselves heroes. As a result, school boards may decide that everything is fine in music education, that our budgets and instructional time are adequate, and they can pat us on the backs while exploring further cuts.

The extreme alternative is to use the test to make a political statement about what kids *aren't* learning in music. If we choose this approach, we hope to prove to legislators and school board members that music educators haven't been provided with the resources needed to teach well. With this as our purpose, we write a test that is rigorous, based on our vision of what children need to learn. Then when kids fail, we point out what we need to do a better

job—time, equipment, and so on.

Somewhere between these two extremes lies an approach that uses tests as diagnostic tools. Such tests, based on a combination of traditional expectations and our vision of what should be learned, focus on analyzing how students are doing in a broad range of areas that we typically teach. The results should enable us to say both where we are doing well and what parts of our programs need to be improved.

Which arts do we assess? We have National Standards in all four arts, even though only two—visual arts and music—are commonly taught in the schools. We can therefore anticipate the question, "What do you *mean* you're going to assess dance? What are you really assessing if hardly anyone has studied dance?" There is little doubt that what most students know about dance would fit in a very small container.

Is it appropriate for students to achieve highly in one art form and less highly in the other art forms? Is proficiency in one art form adequate preparation for life, or do students need more? The National Standards state that students should achieve a broad background in all four arts disciplines and then, at the high school level, go into depth in one art form of their choice. A student may choose music or another art form as his or her in-depth arts area, but can't substitute typing or foreign language. This vision should lead to stronger high school graduation requirements in the arts, because if we expect every child to pursue in-depth study of a selected arts discipline for two years, we must require two credits of high school arts study for graduation. It would be terrific to see that requirement, originally recommended in the federal publication *Toward Civilization,* enacted nationwide.

How authentic can the assessment be? Given the amount of time and money we have to design, administer, and score the test, how much assessing can we do? In a national assessment, you probably would like to have students compose on synthesizers, play guitars, and sing on tape. You might even want to use videotape, so scorers can evaluate students' posture. Such an assessment takes time and money. When looking at the bottom-line cost, it becomes terribly tempting to take the easy route and just hand out that multiple-choice test about Italian definitions.

Which students do we assess? That question has many facets. In a national assessment, which grade levels should we assess? If required music instruction ends in most schools in grade 8—which is still true in Connecticut, but not true in many areas of the country—then maybe we should assess at the end of grade 8. Then perhaps we should also assess students in grade 4, the halfway point to grade 8, and finish up by assessing grade 12, the end point. But isn't it too late to assess in grade 12? Shouldn't we assess in grade 11, so we have at least a year to provide remediation if students don't do well? Even eleventh grade is a little late for corrective action, so should it be grade 10? And so the discussion progresses.

Do we assess every student or just take a sample? This decision certainly affects cost. If the assessment includes lots of performance tasks, then it may not be possible to assess every student. Maybe I will have to assess a random sample, or subset, of the students. In a national assessment, for example, I would assess enough students from each state so I can compare states, and at the state level I would assess enough students so I can compare school districts. At the local level I may want to gather just enough information to compare schools.

In a sampling approach, the sample of students one assesses must include the various subgroups of the general population. For example, you wouldn't want to omit boys, or students with handicaps, or students whose native language is not English. You might therefore take a "probability sample," which means that you decide which groups must be represented and then assess enough students from each of those subgroups to permit a valid comparison.

What content should I assess? Fortunately, we can now turn to the National Standards for some guidance; however, there are quite a few standards. Let's suppose, as is usually true, that

we have limited time and resources. We then have to identify our major concerns, the most important areas about which we need information.

Few people, educators or not, would argue with the fact that singing should be assessed. Although our profession has quite a bit of experience assessing student singing, there are still problems in designing large-scale assessment. If a student sings in a robust gospel style, is that okay? Another sings like "Annie"—is that okay? If the student sings with a head voice like he's been in an Episcopalian boy's choir since birth, is that okay? Can all of those models be acceptable? If the student grew up in Japan, he or she might sing pretty nasally. Is assessing tone therefore "culturally biased?" Then maybe we shouldn't assess tone at all. But if we don't deal with tone, are we not omitting an important quality of music? Listing and training everyone to recognize every acceptable quality will be a big job—we'll get in trouble no matter what we do, but it has to be done.

What about the repertoire these students have studied? Should we expect that all students who studied the music of Japan know those songs published in a certain popular text series? Not all teachers use this series, and some don't use any textbooks at all. Can we make any assumptions about what kids are learning, or should we just decide what *we* think they *should* be learning and test that?

Similar dilemmas present themselves when we consider the assessment of listening to, performing, and creating music. Which repertoire should children be able to analyze? Should we present examples that give them the opportunity to demonstrate what they can do with unfamiliar musical material, and not ask for specific prior knowledge about particular pieces? On what instruments should they be able to play? Should they be competent on one ensemble instrument and one harmonizing instrument? Or should we just expect a certain level of performance, and let the students choose the instrument?

The arts committee of the National Assessment of Educational Progress (NAEP) had to make such choices about the music content appropriate for a national assessment, while still linking its work to the National Standards. The NAEP Framework and Specifications documents would be helpful to anyone designing an assessment at the state or local level, but state and local assessment should measure additional areas of content that cannot be addressed in a national assessment.[5] For example, a state or district could ask teachers to maintain a portfolio of students' music compositions over time, and then check the portfolios periodically to evaluate how the students are doing. A national assessment is a one-shot event, so portfolios are generally out of the question. Districts can also expect students to know a great deal about specific styles or pieces that are part of the local curriculum.

How do you score the assessment? If you don't use a scantron machine, then who decides how successful the students have been? How many teachers am I going to train to score this assessment? This is tremendously valuable in-service training for teachers, so perhaps I should train judges in every state. However, can I provide training that ensures the same standards are applied in Connecticut as in Arizona? Perhaps I need to videotape all of the students' work, bring it into a central office, and have all of the prospective judges sit down and agree on what level of work receives a score of 1, 2, etc.

A related consideration has to do with privacy issues. To assess some aspects of music making, such as singing posture, we may have to videotape the student. Videotaping is *unavoidable* if we are assessing dance and theatre achievement. Will we have to request parental permissions to videotape? Will the tapes be shared or destroyed after the assessment is over? On the one hand, students have a right to privacy. On the other hand, the collection of student performances from a national assessment is a priceless resource for our profession, which might permit us to learn a great deal about students and thereby help us improve our teaching. In the national assessment we might ask parents for permission to retain their students' tapes, and we would

destroy the tapes of those students who don't bring us a signed permission slip (after their performances have been scored).

How high should the stakes be? "Stakes" are the consequences of test performance. Historically, student scores have had consequences primarily for the student. Schools whose students scored well received good publicity, and those whose students didn't score well received bad publicity. Teachers rarely paid any consequences for students doing poorly on tests. Interestingly, music has been a bit of an exception, because some communities have hired and fired their band and choral directors based on how their ensembles scored in rated festivals and competitions. In an outcome-based educational system, tests may take on similar importance for teachers: if students learn, teachers might be rewarded, but if students perform poorly, teachers might be replaced.

Kentucky's school reform process attaches "mega-stakes" to their assessments. After a "baseline" year of measurement that establishes a starting level, schools are expected to show improvement. If a school doesn't perform well, teachers might lose their annual increments and the principal might be replaced; if things still don't improve, both the principals and the teachers could eventually could lose their jobs. On the brighter side, if test scores improve the teachers might receive a pay bonus. In such a system, music must either be a part of the assessment or be left out. What is tested is what is taught.

Individual State Assessments

It is particularly difficult to talk about arts assessment at the state level because states keep changing their minds. With every new governor, there seems to be some kind of new educational reform legislation. States may begin to develop an assessment program, but two years later a new party gains control of the legislature, the economy changes, or the commissioner of education leaves to work for some organization in Washington, D.C., and all plans change.

Illinois started to develop statewide multiple-choice assessment in the arts, but eventually decided to require districts to develop assessment. Vermont started a very exciting project to assess math and writing portfolios, with the intention of getting around to the arts soon thereafter. But they had some trouble getting reliable results in math and writing, so the future is uncertain. They have hired a contractor to work with teachers to design arts assessment and are moving ahead. Maine started an ambitious performance-based art assessment project, but ran aground during the recession. In fact, their very dynamic state arts consultant was reassigned to work in the department of agriculture.

It will come as a surprise to no one that the arts' biggest problem is one of low priority. States typically develop assessment in math, English, science, and social studies first. By the time they get those done, and often by the time they have completed just their math and language arts tests, they have already changed direction. Is there any state that is not assessing students on math, reading, and writing? Of course not. States always get those jobs done first, but they usually fail to get around to the arts.

I left California in 1988. At the time, we had been collecting items for a statewide music test for years. Now, more than six years later, they have completed only a pilot assessment. Minnesota started with ambitious plans, thinking they would assess students in grades 3, 7, and 11 in art and music statewide. They planned a combination of written assessment and performance-based assessment addressing knowledge, history, theory, listening, and performance. They cut a CD of selected repertoire for the music assessment and made a list of artwork for the art assessment. In the spring of 1993 they conducted a sample administration of the test to 5 percent of the students in one third of the state's districts. Then they laid off their arts consultants and offered the test to districts as an optional local assessment.

New York also has an interesting arts assessment project. They have promoted the use of portfolios by running week-long summer in-service institutes for teachers. Recently, I had the opportunity to attend their state music convention, and was impressed with the level of conversation I heard about assessment. The teachers in the room were not saying, "What's a portfolio?" They were saying, "I've been doing portfolios for a year or two. These things are working well. How do I solve this nagging problem, so I can move on to the next step with it?" What seems to be true about portfolio assessment—based on the experiences of Vermont, New York, and other places where it is being done well—is that it transforms the way teachers teach. Focusing on students' final products seems to help teachers rethink and improve their teaching.

State Assessment Consortium (SCASS)

Many states flirt with arts assessment, but have neither the resources nor the commitment to follow through. Hope lies in states pooling their resources so that the impact of high and low cycles of individual state interest in the arts is minimized and collectively a group of states can maintain steady progress in assessment development. The State Collaborative on Assessment and Student Standards (SCASS) project, sponsored by the Council of Chief State School Officers, is attempting to do just that. Because the development stage of a test is extremely expensive, the SCASS allows states to save development costs by pooling resources, then spend money they *do* have on administration and scoring.

Connecticut is participating in the SCASS project. We are in the second phase of the project, during which we have divided into separate working groups that are collecting the best available assessment tasks from all over the country, designing systems and items that might be used for statewide assessment, and designing in-service training programs to help classroom teachers conduct classroom and district-wide assessment in all of the arts. Each state has learned a great deal from this opportunity to discuss its own work and glean ideas from other experts.

Our profession's next step, now that we have written national standards, is to collect examples of student work. Using videotaped examples of students performing the achievement tasks specified in the Standards, we can examine students' work and decide what is "good enough." The videotapes can be a resource for teacher preparation, for communicating with teachers who are working in the schools, and for modeling appropriate musical behaviors for students. We should collaborate to collect these materials, perhaps on a nationwide basis.

Someday, using your classroom computer, you will be able to access these models of quality student work as you design your lesson plans. You'll be able to enter a particular standard and grade level and see students' work, watch quality instruction, and even see teachers conduct various kinds of assessment. Then you'll be better prepared to plan the strategies you plan to use in your own classroom, and you'll be able to compare results with other master teachers.

National Assessment of Educational Progress in the Arts (1997)

The Clinton administration is supporting the arts as one of the core subjects in the nation's education goals. It is also supporting a National Assessment of Educational Progress (NAEP) assessment in the arts in 1997. Some members of congress are questioning the national education goals, and funding has not yet been allocated to administer the 1997 assessment, but at least these problems are not peculiar to the arts.

The purpose of NAEP testing is to get a snapshot of what students across the country know in a particular subject. National assessment in the arts hasn't been done since the 1970s. Earlier arts assessments were designed to measure achievement only in art and music, but the 1997 assessment will test students on their mastery of all four of the visual and performing arts: dance, music, theatre, and the visual arts.

NAEP takes a "probability sampling" approach when deciding which students take the test. This means that, rather than testing every

student and rather than taking a completely random sample of students, NAEP tries to select a representative cross-section of students from all over the country to represent various ethnic groups, students who are from rural and urban schools, students from southern and northern states, and so on. The arts assessment will not collect enough information to compare individual school districts or states, but will allow comparisons by category, such as geographic region.

The 1997 arts NAEP project has three phases. The first phase is the design of the Framework and the Specifications documents.[6] The Framework outlines the content of the field, which means that it is rooted in the new National Standards, and also makes general suggestions about the nature of the assessment. The Specifications document is more technical and specific than the Framework. For example, it gives detailed directions about the types of items that should be developed for each type of music content. This leads into the second phase of the NAEP project, which is to develop the test itself.

Although the nature of a national assessment means that we cannot do some things that we would certainly do on a local level, such as developing portfolios of students' work over time, both the Framework and Specifications documents should be of considerable interest to our field. They contain interesting ideas about the content and assessment of all four arts. The format for NAEP is very interesting and useful, even at the local level. The designers of the assessment chose to measure how well students can demonstrate their mastery of the National Standards by carrying out the three basic artistic processes: *creating* new art, *performing* existing art, and *responding* to art as a member of the audience. All four art disciplines have these categories except visual arts, in which students do not "perform." *Creating* new music includes improvising, composing, and arranging; *performing* existing music includes singing, playing ensemble instruments, and playing harmonizing instruments; and *responding* to music includes acting as an educated listener or consumer. Each of these three processes requires exactly the kind of independent musical thinking that is sought by the advocates of authentic assessment. For example, a student who can independently create music through composing begins by generating alternative ideas, making initial drafts, evaluating and refining each revision, and finally presenting it to others. Assessment at all levels, including the local level, should measure whether students can carry out these processes.

The Future of General Music Assessment

I believe there will be several significant changes in general music assessment. For example, teachers will collect student portfolios by digitizing students' work and storing it on computers. The material in the folders will be evaluated using scoring systems based on the National Standards. Portfolios will include compositions, improvisations, and written work such as critiques of music and performances, as well as the more traditional performances.

Teachers will use more visual components in instruction, such as those increasingly available on CD-ROMs. This will enable them to teach more effectively by presenting, for example, visual information about the cultural context of the works to which their students listen. Publishers will include prepackaged visual aids to accompany their music and text series, including video examples of students working with those materials. These will prove useful both in providing a model for students and for setting standards when evaluating students.

The report cards of the future will consist of files that teachers put on-line for parents to review. Music teachers will select samples of their students' work to attach to their video explanation of the students' progress, which parents will be able to call up on their home screen. Parents will be able to compare their student's work to exemplary models, review the curriculum on screen, and see what their student will be studying next. Parents will also have the option of requesting a video telephone conference with the teacher about their student's work.

Until this not-so-futuristic day arrives, each

local music faculty should, as part of their curriculum development process, design district-wide assessment based on projects that every teacher should have students complete at certain grade levels. Teachers should collect the results of these projects in a portfolio for each student. The portfolio projects should be designed to demonstrate students' mastery of the outcomes outlined in the local music curriculum, which is, we hope, aligned with our new National Standards. Each student's portfolio should include at least an audio recording of the student's performances, improvisations, and compositions, as well as written work, such as analyses and critiques of music works and performances studied in class. Local districts should use these portfolios to conduct district-wide evaluations of students' music achievement. Districts must acquire the technology to permit development of student portfolios, and provide music teachers with the time to manage the portfolios. If time is limited, then so must be the number of projects completed and collected.

States must continue to develop assessments that will hold all schools accountable for teaching students music and the other arts. Portfolios should probably play a role in the state assessment process. In fact, states may begin to outline some basic expectations for what should be included in local portfolios, and sample those portfolios periodically to ensure that districts are providing students with a quality music education. I hope to see such a system included in our new Connecticut curriculum framework. MENC and state departments of education should also help practitioners design local assessments linked to their local curricula.

General music learning can and must be assessed. Think deeply about what types of learning are most important in your curriculum. Discuss with your colleagues authentic ways to assess that learning, making sure that you ask students to carry out the three artistic processes. Choose one assessment idea to try first, perhaps while a colleague tries a different idea. Compare notes. Compare students' work. Repeat the process to design assessments that address other areas of your curriculum. As you develop effective assessment strategies, begin to build them into your curriculum guide. Report the results to your community. Use the results to improve your program. In short, use assessment to make your teaching, and therefore your students' learning, more successful.

Notes

1. Richard Colwell, *Music Achievement Tests 1 and 2* (Chicago: Follett Educational Corporation, 1967).

2. Edwin E. Gordon, *Iowa Tests of Music Literacy* (Iowa City: Bureau of Educational Research and Service, University of Iowa, 1970); *Primary Measures of Music Audiation* (Chicago: GIA Publications, 1979); and *Intermediate Measures of Music Audiation* (Chicago: GIA Publications, 1982).

3. S. Farnum and J. Watkins, *The Watkins-Farnum Performance Scale* (Winona, MN: Harold Leonard, Inc., 1954).

4. Richard Colwell, *Silver Burdett Music Competency Tests* (Morristown, NJ: Silver Burdett, 1979).

5. The College Board, *1996 NAEP Arts Education Assessment and Exercise Specifications* (Washington, DC: National Assessment Governing Board, 1994, prepublication edition).

6. The College Board, *1996 NAEP Arts Education Assessment Framework* (Washington, DC: National Assessment Governing Board, 1994, prepublication edition).

Music educators acknowledge that assessment in the general music classroom has become an important issue in education reform. To many teachers, however, the transition from awareness of assessment issues and information to practice and implementation of assessment strategies in the classroom remains difficult. Jennifer Davidson, with the assistance of teachers in the Waterford (Michigan) School District, shows how elementary and middle school general music educators can develop and use assessment strategies relevant and meaningful to local programs. Information about the videotape that was part of this presentation can be found at the end of the article.

Assessment in General Music
So Where Do I Start?

By Jennifer Davidson

Assessment is being discussed by educators across America. To bring this topic into sharp focus for general music teachers, two sessions on assessment were planned for the September 1993 National General Music Symposium. Scott Shuler and I, music cochairs of the 1997 National Assessment of Education Programs Arts Consensus Project, were invited to present the assessment sessions. We decided on these two presentations:

■ Information about assessment projects currently underway at the state and national levels (see Scott Shuler's article, page 51).

■ A focus on assessment in the general music classroom.

My presentation would cover the latter, and I was fortunate to have colleagues in the nearby Waterford (Michigan) School District who were implementing basic assessment strategies. We met to talk about their work and to consider options for sharing their ideas at a national conference.

Jennifer Davidson is the arts education consultant for the Oakland Intermediate School District in Oakland County, Michigan.

As Scott and I continued our meetings on the NAEP project, we speculated about possible levels of assessment awareness on the part of general music teachers. We came up with four:

Level 1: "Yes, I've heard the word."

Level 2: "I've been to a few workshops and read a few articles, and I have a general idea what assessment is about."

Level 3: "I've read and studied about assessment, and I've tried a few strategies with my students in my music classes."

Level 4: "I've been working on assessment strategies in general music for some time now, and I'm ready to present workshops for my fellow teachers."

We surmised that the difficult part is getting teachers from level two to level three. There are, in fact, many teachers out there who are somewhat familiar with the idea of assessment but are not sure where to begin the process with their students in general music.

The Waterford teachers and I decided that our goal for the symposium presentation would be to demonstrate ways to begin using assessment strategies in music class; that is, moving from level two to level three. We decided to create a video that would show participants at the Symposium the ways that the two Waterford teachers had begun to implement assessment strategies with their students. In May 1993 we shot about twenty-five hours of source tape of the Waterford teachers with four general music classes at grades 1, 5, 7, and 8. In addition, I interviewed both teachers, their supervisor, and about thirty of their students. Over the summer we created a video to show at the symposium in Reston. What follows is the narration for that twenty-five minute video (minus the students' comments, live action of students making music and assessing their work, and the teacher interviews):

Jackie Thompson is a successful general music teacher in Michigan. Like her colleagues around the country, she is aware that a new word has crept into common usage among all of us who are educators. No matter where we turn in education these days, the word "assessment" seems to crop up. Music teachers have encountered the word as they attend faculty meetings, look at professional journals, and read newspaper articles about current issues affecting schools.

But few workshops, teacher in-service meetings, or articles deal directly with assessment in the general music classroom. Although many music teachers are aware of the term "assessment" and have read a little about portfolios and authentic assessment, they are often unsure as to how to implement new assessment strategies in their own classes.

The purpose of this video presentation is to look at two general music teachers who took the leap, who decided on their own to consider the implications of assessment in general music, and to see what it meant with their students.

The first teacher is Jackie Thompson, an elementary general music specialist who works with nine hundred students in three schools. She sees each class for a half hour each week.

Julia Kohring is a middle school music teacher who meets five classes each day. She sees her general music students for fifty minutes a day for ten weeks.

Both of these teachers are part of the Waterford School District, a middle-class area in suburban Detroit. The school district has a pop-ulation of approximately twelve thousand students. Fifteen years ago the elementary music program was cut for financial reasons. The cut lasted five years. The district, at this point, has finally overcome the damage done by that cut.

Both of these teachers have taught for several years and are regarded as successful by their colleagues. Why did they choose to learn more about assessment and implement new strategies and techniques into their teaching?

This past year Jackie started two assessment projects: one with her fifth graders and one with her first graders.

In the fifth grade the students developed their own criteria for evaluating their singing and musical performances. This grew out of the need for a Grandparents' Day program. Jackie was concerned that she not stop teaching her regular curriculum in order to have something to present for the special program. She designed an "informance" that would allow the children to share with their grandparents what they had learned about Beethoven, rondo form, and choral singing. The students were delighted with the opportunity to design their own project in music, to decide what learning was important, and to determine what areas needed improvement.

Jackie's first-grade project revolved around singing skills. Her assessment work was designed to help children determine on their own if they were learning to match pitch, rather than always having the teacher tell them if they were singing in tune. The children were recorded over a two-year period. At each session the students were asked to assess how well they were doing and if they could hear improvement. In the video, the children's faces often tell as much as their words.

Julia's seventh-grade general music curriculum used a composition unit to teach note reading, music vocabulary, structural elements, and basic composition skills.

For this past year, Jackie and Julia have both focused on new ways of looking at learning in general music. In addition to teacher observation, their one traditional means of assessing learning, they have now added several new strategies to their assessment repertoire. After piloting new assessment models in general music, there are six questions to consider:

1. How do your administrators respond to your work in this area?

2. Have you been able to assess students' values and attitudes as well as their skills and knowledge?

3. Are the students different in any way as a result of this new emphasis on alternative means of assessing learning?

4. If one of the primary goals of teaching is to empower students to be lifelong learners, have they been successful at learning to "self-assess"?

5. What changes do you plan for next year?

6. What suggestions would you offer a teacher who would like to implement new assessment strategies?

If general music teachers are to remain viable players on the faculty, they must heed the state-ment of a member of the Michigan Board of Education: "What is assessed is what will remain in the curriculum." We must be able to demonstrate, beyond the traditional means of concerts, what students are learning about music. For our own sakes, and more important, for our students, we must implement new ways of having students own what they are learning. We must give them the tools to know when to practice or think through an idea again, and when to move on to something new. Our future as music educators and the future of our students depend on it.

Following the video presentation, the two teachers and the supervisor from the Waterford Schools answered questions from conference participants.

Copies of the video are available for $10.00 from Linda Erkkila, Video Services, Oakland Schools, 2100 Pontiac Lake Road, Waterford, MI 48328.

Changes in attitudes that lead toward acceptance of diversity begin in classrooms in which cultural uniqueness is discovered and valued through study of the arts. In support of this position, Marvelene C. Moore examines the role of the arts and issues of authenticity when music of non-Western origins becomes part of the general music curriculum. From the earliest forms of spirituals to singing games to contemporary rap music, Moore cites characteristics of African American music that cross genres and historical eras. She argues for authenticity in performance practice that will convey to students the richness of the cultural mosaic in which they live.

Cultural Diversity and Music
Authenticity in Performance

By Marvelene C. Moore

The American society is and has always been a diverse, multicultural one. But over the past two decades something new has emerged. We have become more visibly diverse due in part to the influx of new immigrants—from Africa, the Caribbean, the Middle East, India, and a greater percentage than before from Asia and Latin America. We have become a more colorful people. But the diversity that some of us celebrate represents problems to others—it constitutes, in the eyes of some people, frightening, unwanted changes in our society. The American ideal for most citizens is a monocultural society that combines its many cultures into one culture, one language, one purpose, one people—"the melting pot." Despite the fact that the United States has always been a diverse multicultural society, we Americans have not really accepted it.[1]

How then do we bring about the necessary change in attitude and in reality? The school is the place where the process can begin, where children can learn and come to believe that what they have been taught by their parents has a place or is of value in the society. The classroom is an ideal place for representing the uniqueness

Marvelene C. Moore is professor of music education at the University of Tennessee, Knoxville.

of various cultures through exposure to and study of the arts.

As we contemplate a new vision for general music and preparing students to meet the challenges of the twenty-first century, we need to look more closely at the role of the arts. Harold Williams, president and chief executive officer of the J. Paul Getty Trust, believes that "the arts are basic and a central medium to human communication and understanding. The arts are how we talk to each other. They are the language of civilization—past and present—through which we express our anxieties, our hungers, our hopes, and our discoveries. They are our means of listening to our dreams—of expressing our imagination and feeling."[2]

The arts reaffirm our humanity. They are the glue that holds society together. While improvements in the three "Rs" may enable us to compete more effectively in the world economically and technologically, they do not free the human spirit, which is basic to our existence. As Charles Fowler has said, "Apple (computer) is technology and the arts should be at the core." Too much emphasis is placed on the three "Rs" to the exclusion of the arts. The National Endowment for the Arts has recognized this problem in its final report, which states that "the artistic heritage that is ours and the opportunities to contribute significantly to its evolution are being lost to our young people."[3] Not only does the absence or meagerness of the arts in our schools deny children access to the vast treasure of American and world cultures, but without the arts we are not replenishing our infrastructure to assure the cultural future of the country.

Recently politicians and administrators have begun to be more vocal about the importance of the arts in the education of children. Assemblywoman Maureen Ogden of New Jersey believes that "when you compare two similar schools, one with a strong arts curriculum and one without, you will soon discover that there are nonartistic benefits that make the schools with arts higher performance environments. Most important, in such settings the students are excited about learning."[4]

President Bush remarked at the opening of the Kazimir Malevich Exhibition that "fine arts transcend differences in language and culture, providing a bridge between peoples that fosters better understanding among nations."[5]

These leaders believe that the arts do change lives, that our children will grow and develop through the arts, creating changes in their own lives and the lives of people around them. An effective way of achieving change in attitudes and in appreciating and understanding people who make up our neighborhoods, communities, states, nations, and the world is through the study of a culture's art and, for our purpose, specifically through its music. In order to understand a culture's music, the characteristics and features unique to its music must be experienced. In other words, the music must be experienced in an authentic way.

For some years now I have been concerned about the presentation of music from various cultural groups in performance and in performance materials. As a matter of fact, my doctoral dissertation deals with the subject of "authenticity" in performance of music from the African American and Native American cultures. I found that in most cases the music of these two cultures was altered melodically and rhythmically and that inappropriate body movements and

instrumentation were recommended to accompany the songs.

Webster's New Collegiate Dictionary (1976) defines authenticity as "not imaginary or false, conforming to an original so as to reproduce essential features, without counterfeiting, admixture, or adulteration." Performance is defined as "a public presentation or exhibition." An authentic performance in music may be described then as a public presentation that is not imaginary or false (to the culture) but conforms to the original (to the music culture—past or present) so as to reproduce essential features (concepts, styles, expressive qualities of the music) without counterfeiting, admixture, or adulteration. That means that the music, when presented as authentic, should not be altered to fit another's sound orientation, to suit our personal performance preference for the sake of teaching skills or concepts, to satisfy our traditions, or for entertainment purposes. To alter the music in any of those ways would result in transforming the music to suit our tastes, promoting the melting-pot theory in the presentation of the music.

In looking at the spiritual "Sinner Man" from the African American culture, frequently paired with the sea shanty "Drunken Sailor," we find inappropriate application of the spiritual. The African spiritual is a style of a religious nature sung for special occasions and for special reasons; that is, it was based on religion or events in the bible, used to carry secret messages of escape plans to freedom, performed in church or at religious settings, frequently accompanied by hand clapping and foot stomping, and not paired with other songs for the sake of producing harmony. So to pair "Sinner Man" with "Drunken Sailor" is to ignore what we know about the African spiritual by pairing it (as a partner song) with a drinking song.

In looking more closely at various styles of African American music, we find that there are specific music characteristics that make it unique:

■ The music is usually performed in duple meter; triple meter is rare

■ Syncopation is almost always present

■ The "blue note" is used extensively for variety in sound and for expressive purposes

■ Melodies are usually pentatonic and can be major or minor

■ The form of the melodies is often call and response

These characteristics have their roots in the music of Africa and are found in every style of African American music.

Two examples are "Josephine" and "Way Go Lily," African American singing games that were sung by children before the turn of the century. These songs are typical of African American music: duple meter, syncopation, pentatonic, and body percussion as accompaniment.

A popular song of my youth, "Jump Back Baby," is the example. In addition to the characteristics found in the singing games, it is an excellent example of call and response.

Gospel music is a very popular medium of the twentieth century. It is reminiscent of the spiritual in its religious nature and in the message of hope and joy that it carries. The example "What A Mighty God We Serve," by the Los Angeles Mass Choir, speaks about joy and hope in its reference to singing, clapping, dancing, and shouting before the Lord. When singing it, the movements that are mentioned in the text are generally performed.

Rap music is a contemporary African American music form. Much controversy surrounds the use of rap in the music classroom because of the language that many deem unacceptable. Regardless of our opinions about rap music, it is imperative that we look carefully for those examples that are suitable for the classroom. As we listen to the radio, watch television, listen to music that serves as background for movies, and so on, we see that rap permeates every facet of our society. It is necessary, then, for music teachers to include this music from the culture in classroom instruction. Jane Healy put it very succinctly when she stated that today's students reject concepts and ideas that are not relevant to their experience. Rap is experienced by most young people in our society and by

youth in other parts of the world. The song "Jump, Jump," by Kriss Kross, is an excellent example of a rap composition that embodies all of the music features that characterize African American music. To perform music labeled as African American that does not reflect these basic features nor suggest the appropriate style of performance would distract from the uniqueness of the music. Further it would misrepresent the culture's music and sound foreign to the students from the culture who participate in the music on a daily basis.

I hope that I have impressed upon you in some way the necessity for incorporating music of many cultures into the music curriculum, the importance of performing music that is characteristic of the particular culture, and the necessity for authenticity in performance practice. The benefits to our students are multidimensional. They will acquire new musical experiences, acquire an appreciation for diversity, actively participate in different ways of making music, develop understanding of indigenous music groups, and develop a tolerance and respect for people of other cultures, which we hope will lead to changing attitudes and developing friendships. If we accomplish these goals, we will truly convey to our students that our country and the world is not a melting pot. Rather, it is a mosaic that requires their existence to make the picture complete.

Notes

1. Lily Wong Fillmore. "Educating Citizens," *Multicultural Education* (San Francisco: Caddo Gap Press, Summer 1993).

2. Harold Williams. "The Language of Civilization: The Vital Role of the Arts in Education," Plenary Meeting XXIV of the President's Committee on the Arts and the Humanities (New York: Century Association, 1991), p. 1.

3. See Williams, p. 4.

4. See Williams, p. 5.

5. See Williams, p. 1.

Ellen McCullough-Brabson advocates an inclusive perspective for defining music and justifying its place in the school curriculum. Each individual, she states, has a musical culture associated with life experiences and rituals. Study that leads to respect for various world musics may also bring about respect for the people who created them. McCullough-Brabson reviews the questions and issues music educators consider as they begin to include world musics in the curriculum. She encourages us to challenge our own ideas, allow ourselves to perceive the world differently, and to be open to new sounds in our classrooms and our lives.

Music and Cultural Diversity
Thoughts from a
World Music Cheerleader

By Ellen McCullough-Brabson

"Sorida!" "Hello, Everybody!" "Dipidu!" "Bonjour, Mes Amis!" "Funga Alafia!" "Hello! Hello! Hello!" Elementary general music students sing a colorful mosaic of greeting songs from around the world, including the ones above. These musical expressions of "hello" clearly illustrate cultural diversity. Although we may communicate our "hello" in different languages, it is common for humans to greet each other in some fashion. It is also common for each culture to express itself musically through a rich smorgasbord of exciting sounds.

Many music educators embrace the premise that music is a human universal. Some important questions still remain, however. Why should we include world music in our teaching? Do we all have a musical culture? Which music should we teach? How do we teach world music? In addition, the effects that world music and cultural diversity may have on the future direction of music education must be addressed.

Ellen McCullough-Brabson is professor of music education at the University of New Mexico in Albuquerque.

In 1967 the Tanglewood Symposium examined the issues of music education and world music. Its directive was that multicultural music should be included in the American school curriculum. It is decades later and this point is still a major issue for many music educators. Again the question is asked, "Why world music?" A possible answer to this inquiry can be found in a familiar folk tale from India. The following synopsis is an adaption of this amusing story.

There once were seven blind mice. One day they discovered a new creature by their pond. They decided to go to the pond one at a time to figure out what it could possibly be. The first mouse felt the leg of the object and decided it must be a pillar; the second felt the trunk of the object and concluded it was a snake; the third felt the tusk of the thing and knew that it had to be a spear; the fourth mouse crawled on the head of the monstrosity and discovered it was a cliff; the fifth sat upon the ear and verified it was a fan; and the sixth rodent swung on the tail and swore it was a rope. When the six mice shared their analysis of the creature, they began to argue. They could not come to a conclusion. So the seventh mouse scampered to the pond and touched the object from head to toe. It discovered that the creature did, indeed, seem like a pillar, a snake, a spear, a cliff, a fan, and a rope; however, when all the parts were put together the seventh mouse knew that it had to be an elephant. The mouse moral was very clear: "Knowing in part may make a fine tale, but wisdom comes from seeing the whole."[1]

Following the moral of this tale, an inclusive veiwpoint needs to be taken when defining music and justifying its inclusion in the school curriculum. An exclusive way of teaching music is not fully representative of what music is, and it only allows us to know one part. There are many types of music, not just Western art music. We need to see the whole picture of what music is. In her article "Is Western Art Music Superior?" ethnomusicologist Judith Becker argues that all musics are worthy of study.[2] Aesthetic experiences and "goosebump moments" are not just reserved for the cultural elite—all humans respond to music. It is time for music educators to define music inclusively and to provide world music experiences to students in their classrooms. To use only one kind of music in the classroom is to see only one part of the elephant, rather than the complete whole. The study of world music can help us define what music is: a worldwide human phenomenom.

Before world music can be embraced by music educators, some difficult and soul-searching questions need to be asked. A good starting point is, "Do we all have a musical culture?" I would answer that question with an emphatic yes. But not all of us may think so. For example, I once had a student who described an experience she had just had in a university education methods course. She said that they examined cultural roots and that many of her fellow students had described exotic and exciting cultures. Their descriptions included images of interesting and vivid costumes, dances, songs, and foods. She deeply lamented that she did not have a culture and that she sure wished that she did. I was shocked. We all have cultures, even Anglo-Americans!

That story raises many issues about culture:

What is cultural diversity? Who am I? What is my culture? What is my ethnicity? What is my musical culture? Do I have cultural roots? What is my genealogy? What songs did my great-grandmother or great-grandfather sing? What songs did my parents and grandparents sing? What dances did they dance? Should children have a sense of their own cultural roots? Will their sense of cultural identity develop a positive self-esteem? I am an Anglo-American. Do I want to be called Euro-American, Anglo, white, or some other term? Do I first consider myself a human being and then an American and then a person with a special identity and then a wife and mother and then a music educator? What is the ordering of my world and how do I fit in culture? How would I describe my musical culture to a Klingon from "Star Trek: The Next Generation?" What songs and dances would I include?

The preceding questions are often difficult ones to answer. But before we can examine other cultures and their music, perhaps it would be good to start in our own backyards. When looking at our own musical cultures, it may be beneficial to consider the musical events of our lives. What music is associated with life rituals? What music is performed at birthdays, baptisms, graduation ceremonies, sporting events, weddings, funerals, and holidays? What is our musical culture? Although the answers may be complex and diverse, responding to these questions can help us learn about our own musical culture and about other cultures as well.

At an even deeper level, world music educators should project a very special sensitivity to other cultures. Will they continue to laugh at ethnic jokes that are hurtful? Will they display prejudice? Or will respect for world music lead them to respect the people who create that music? And most important, will the students they teach reflect this attitude, too?

Other frequently asked questions are, "If I use world music in my classroom, which music should I teach? How can I teach all of the music from around the world? Do I have to give up my Kodály, Orff, or Dalcroze training to embrace this music?" I am reminded of a favorite childhood poem that my grandfather read to me from the McGuffy Reader. It began, "Which shall it be? Which shall it be? I looked at John, and John looked at me."[3] The storyline of the poem describes a mother and father who have a family of seven children. They are very poor. One day they receive a letter from a wealthy man who said that he would give them a house and land in exchange for one of their children. As they looked at each child sleeping that night, they knew they would remain in poverty. Each child was far too precious to give away for any price.

Music educators face serious dilemmas and choices regarding world music in their classroom. For some teachers, it becomes an either/or decision, just like the poem. Which shall it be? Shall I use my Kodály training? If so, can I still incorporate world music? Will I have to give up my Western art music training and my teaching of Western art music in order to embrace world musics? Certainly not. According to Patricia Shehan Campbell, world music can be connected to any music education method.[4]

Another issue regarding which music to teach involves the question of breadth and depth. Should I examine one world music in depth for a year or should I do a mini world-music survey? Which of these approaches would be most beneficial to my students? Will I be considered a charlatan if I only briefly examine the music of another culture? Will it not take several lifetimes to know as much as I need to know about another culture? Is one lifetime long enough to teach world music? Is one lifetime long enough to know my own musical culture? How can I be skilled enough to teach world music? If I only know three songs from that culture and one listening lesson, is that enough or is it superficial? Bruno Nettl addressed many of these questions at the International Society for Music Education conference in Seoul, South Korea. He stated, "The idea is not to teach the music of these cultures, and for students to know them, but to teach something about them and for students to know they exist and are worthy of attention and

respect. Emphatically, it is better to know a little than nothing. The first thing our students need to get is a sense of what's out there."[5]

Once music educators are committed to including world music in their curriculum, they want to know how to get started. As the Chinese proverb states, the thousand-mile journey begins with the first step. Here are some typical questions music educators ask:

How will I find materials? The music education world-music materials market has come a long way since the days when a song might be labeled "Song from Africa" with no translation or additional information regarding where it came from within Africa. Many wonderful sources are available through MENC and presses that feature world music. These materials include superior listening tapes and teacher guides with excellent information about the selected music and culture.

Do I have to be a trained ethnomusicologist to use world music in my classroom? The answer is no. There are many wonderful resources written by ethnomusicologists and world-music educators that present the material effectively. Music educators need to continue to wear the hat of music educators. Connections are being made between the two fields so that the music educator will not have to be an expert in both disciplines. In fact, current world-music materials are designed to be user-friendly.

What about process and product? Are children playing in an Orff ensemble tuned to a Balinese gamelan really learning about Balinese culture? I once asked my gamelan instructor from Java what he thought about this. He replied that Orff gamelans were just fine as long as the students knew that they were playing an Orff gamelan and not the real thing. How much can a student really learn by playing in such an ensemble? Can a student capture the musical spirit of the culture? Can those who study world music ever truly be cultural insiders or will they always be cultural outsiders? It is a puzzle to find the balance. Who owns a song anyway? When you hear a song on the playground is the child the owner of the song or is the person who taught the song the owner?

Do I need to be a social studies teacher to teach world music? No, but because music is an integral part of any culture, a complete picture of music should be given by either the music teacher or the social studies teacher or both. For example, information about the geography, history, language, economy, politics, family life, holidays, customs, education, arts, and music of a culture can tell us much about the culture and can make our understanding more complete. Music is integrated with life, it is not a separate entity.

Many other issues of how to teach world music need to be addressed. The following ideas are suggested tips for successful teaching.

■ Use the language of the culture. Although this may take a tremendous amount of work, it is well worth it. Translations often cannot capture the spirit of the music or the exact meaning or sounds integral to the lyrics.

■ Provide translations. Children always want to know what the words of songs mean. I once had a student who would not sing the Anglo-American song "Pawpaw Patch" until he knew what a pawpaw was. His mother told him never to use words he did not understand.

■ Use authentic materials. Bruno Nettl said that ethnomusicologists defined authenticity out of existence in the early 1950's. His point was that ethnomusicologists accept what is. Change is the only certain thing we know. Nettl also states, "If there is anything really stable in the musics of the world, it is the constant existence of change. The one thing that perhaps unites all musicological endeavor—and possibly all humanistic and social disciplines—is the need to understand this constant of humanity."[6]

Music educators are really concerned with authenticity. They do not want to share a cultural song unless it is truly from that culture. In many instances, teachers have to take a leap of faith and hope the materials they have selected are accurate. I have also heard music educators say that they want music to remain pure and unchanged. Their intent may be honorable because they would like to preserve the past and

musical traditions. Change, however, is going to happen. There will be musical mixes whenever cultures interact. In the 1960s, a phrase was coined that described how to analyze the educational system. It was called "crap-detecting." All world-music educators must be good "crap-detectors." They must carefully examine world-music materials and use their best judgment to discover representative music materials. Another point to consider is that not all members of a cultural group will perform music from their culture in exactly the same way.

■ Know the cultural context. Who traditionally performs this song? Do both boys and girls sing the song or is it gender specific? Is it only sung during certain times of the year or is it performed year-long? Is the song associated with a ritual or holiday? Is it performed only at a certain time of day, afternoon, or evening?

■ Develop respect for other cultures. Is the music associated with a ritual or ceremony? If so, is it appropriate for an outsider of the culture to sing it or dance it? Should the music be performed outside of the cultural context?

■ Avoid words with negative stereotyping. For example, the song "Taffy" has lyrics that are stereotyped and negative ("Taffy was a Welshman, Taffy was a thief."). Should this song be performed?

■ Know the meaning of songs. Are there social values or norms connected with the music? In *Let Your Voice Be Heard!* the authors describe how the song "Sansa Kroma" teaches children of Ghana not to worry if they are accidentally orphaned. They will be taken care of by their community.

■ Sing in the vocal style of the culture. Do all cultural groups sing with a Westernized, relaxed, and open voice? Will singing with a different singing style hurt your voice? Although more research needs to be done in this area, many music educators agree that the answers to those questions are no. A real cultural crossover occurs when singing style changes. This topic is certainly an exciting new avenue for discussion.

Music educators have a great challenge ahead of them as they face the future and the twenty-first century. One wonders if the same or similar discussions will be taking place one hundred years from now. For music educators who want to be involved with world music in their classrooms, here are some suggested directions:

■ A "Survey of World Music" class needs to be mandated for undergraduate music majors. University students must have an inclusive view of what music is. If they have such a class, they will have a good background for teaching world music in their classrooms. Our culture reflects diversity, yet we are still closeted with Western art music. Other creative curricula could be designed, too. For example, I teach a multicultural music class for elementary classroom teachers. It examines the social studies and world-music curriculum connection. Although the focus is on teaching world music, an integrated viewpoint is highlighted.

■ MENC must take the initiative and offer in-depth summer study courses led by ethnomusicologists and world-music educators. Classes could be offered at selected sites around the country. Perhaps one site could focus on African music, one on African-American music, one on Latin-American music, one on Asian-American music, one on Native American music, and so on.

■ All-state conferences in each of the fifty states should include multicultural music workshops for their yearly sessions. MENC could help supply clinicians and speakers. Music educators need to interact with people from another culture. A highlight for me has been my association with my Navajo students. They have generously shared with me their songs, their stories, and their customs.

■ Teachers should also be encouraged to listen to as much recorded music from selected cultures as possible. These materials may be the very best authentic and representative music resources from that culture.

■ There is also much to be said for attending as many live performances as possible. They can provide incredible goosebump moments. In Albuquerque last year, the Pueblo Indian Cultural Center sponsored a culturally diverse musical program for its Father's Day celebration. The lineup of performers looked like a mini United Nations concert. The program featured traditional American Indian hoop dances, bagpipers, Hispanic singers and dancers, Peruvian music, Hawaiian dancers, and the Chinese ribbon and chopstick dance. What a beautiful gift to the community!

■ World-music educators should watch videos that feature different cultures. Television specials are often great resources for cultural information, too.

■ Technological advances will continue to impact the teaching of world musics. For example, CD-ROMs are our future. Two examples of this new technology are "Musical Instruments from around the World" and "The Global Jukebox" created by Alan Lomax. I predict that technological advances will allow our students to bring a culture into the classroom with great ease. Perhaps our students will only have to click a button and there will be cultural interaction. Maybe there will be CD-ROM titles such as "Celebrations from around the World" or "Songs of Greeting from around the World" or "Circle Dances from around the World."

■ Music educators should consider joining the Society for Ethnomusicology. It has an education component that provides ethnomusicology and music education sessions on Saturday mornings of their conferences.

■ Teachers should attend the International Society for Music Education (ISME) international conferences. They provide many stimulating performances, papers, and workshops. ISME is also an excellent venue to meet music educators from around the world. There is no doubt that world-music educators are also risk-takers. It takes lots of courage to sing songs in different languages, to insist the the music we present is accurate and representative, to question the cultural context of the material we present, to challenge the idea that Western art music is superior, to advocate that the children we teach have the right to hear music from around the world. The only way children may learn to perceive the world differently and to become open-minded when they hear new sounds is to be exposed to multicultural musics. We can give a tremendous gift to the children we teach. The gift is to allow them to experience how music works and how it contributes to that which makes us, and the rest of the world, human.

Can listening to world music open our hearts to understanding the people who make the music? Marilyn Hood, a Navajo musician, described the benefits of taking a multicultural music class. The song she remembered the most was "Sakura," a Japanese folk song. She sang it to her five children every night before they went to bed. She also became more curious about other American Indian songs for the first time in her life.

In Robert Fulghum's book, *All I Really Need to Know I Learned in Kindergarten*, he states that the greatest word of all is "Look!" Although music educators would agree that "look" is a powerful word, we understand and know that the most dynamic word of all is really "Listen!"

Notes

1. Ed Young, *Seven Blind Mice* (New York: Philomel Books, 1992), 36.

2. Judith Becker, "Is Western Art Music Superior?" *Musical Quarterly* 72, 1986, 341–59.

3. *McGuffey's Fourth Eclectic Reader* (New York: Van Nostrand Reinhold Company, Inc., 1920), 168–71.

4. Patricia Campbell, "Cultural Consciousness in Teaching General Music," *Music Educators Journal* 78, No. 9 (May 1992): 30–36.

5. Bruno Nettl, "Ethnomusicology and the Teaching of World Music," *International Journal of Music Education* No. 20, 1992, 5.

6. Bruno Nettl, *The Study of Ethnomusicology* (Urbana, IL: University of Illinois Press, 1983), 174.

Selected Bibliography

Anderson, William M. "Toward a Multicultural Future," *Music Educators Journal* 77, No. 9 (May 1991): 29–31.

Becker, Judith. "Is Western Art Music Superior?" *Musical Quarterly* 72, 341–59.

Billman, Jane. "The Native American Curriculum: Attempting Alternatives for Tepees and Headbands," *Young Children* 47, No. 6 (September 1992): 22–25.

Campbell, Patricia Shehan. "Cultural Consciousness in Teaching General Music," *Music Educators Journal* 78, No. 9 (May 1992): 30–36.

Gonzo, Carroll. "Multicultural Issues in Music Education," *Music Educators Journal* (February 1993): 49–52.

Koeppel, Janis and Moe Mulrooney. "The Sister Schools Program: A Way for Children to Learn About Cultural Diversity—When There Isn't Any in Their School," *Young Children* 48, No. 1 (November 1992): 44–47.

Lipson, Greta and Jane Romatowski. *Ethnic Pride* (Carthage, IL: Good Apple, Inc., 1983).

McAllester, David P. *Becoming Human through Music* (Reston, VA: Music Educators National Conference, 1985).

Nettl, Bruno. "Ethnomusicology and the Teaching of World Music," *International Journal of Music Education* 20 (1992): 3–8.

Nettl, Bruno. *The Study of Ethnomusicology* (Urbana, IL: University of Illinois Press, 1983).

Palmer, Anthony J. "World Musics in Music Education: The Matter of Authenticity," *International Journal of Music Education* 19 (1992): 32–40.

Reimer, Bennett. "Music Education in Our Multimusical Culture," *Music Educators Journal* 79, No. 7 (March 1993): 21–26.

Seeger, Anthony. "Celebrating the American Music Mosaic," *Music Educators Journal* 78, No. 9 (May 1992): 26–29.

Volk, Terese M. "The History and Development of Multicultural Music Education as Evidenced in the *Music Educators Journal*, 1967–1992," *Journal of Research in Music Education* 41, No. 2 (1993): 137–55.

More than a quarter century after the Tanglewood Symposium declaration encouraged music educators to expand the school music repertoire, notes Will Schmid, challenges to including diverse musics in the curriculum remain. While awareness of musical diversity has increased and resources are more available, the profession continues to seek frameworks and vocabulary to help us make "sense out of what we hear, play, and compose." Schmid provides an outline for examining what music is and how it is organized as a starting point for including diverse musics in the general music curriculum.

If All, Then What?
What to Teach in a Musically Diverse World

By Will Schmid

How can K–12 general music teachers and university teacher educators make sense out of the increasingly diverse musics that constitute today's world of music?

When I began teaching instrumental, choral, and general music in 1962, the assumed canon of music literature was European classical music and the folk music of Europe and America. College course work in music history and literature—then as now—almost exclusively covered European classical music with the assumption that folk music was simple enough for any trained musician to understand. Non-Western music, jazz, and popular music were often treated by students as a form of "underground" music since they were not given serious attention or curricular time. The word multicultural was not used, and concepts of world or global thinking were the sole province of seers like Marshall McLuhan.

A lot has happened in the past thirty years to change this picture, and yet some things remain the same. The decade of the 1960s changed American society in many ways, and it had a substantial impact on the repertoire of music studied in schools. The doors of musical style were flung wide open to rock and popular as well as world musics. The Tanglewood Symposium of 1967 threw down the gauntlet taken up a year later by the Youth Music Project, and school music has not been the same since. During the past twenty-five years, textbook and sheet-music publishers have gradually included more diverse musics in their catalogs so that today's music teacher is presented with a veritable smorgasbord of possibilities.

One regrettable negative in the midst of this positive change is that the university music history and literature curriculum for most newly certified music teachers does not require any courses in non-Western music or American folk and popular music. Although such course work is increasingly available as an elective on many university campuses, the core of study is still the Grout History of Western Music. As a result of this kind of narrow education, young teachers are left with a "Renaissance–Baroque–Classical–Romantic" way of processing such diverse musics as blues, African drumming, Indonesian gamelan, or Indian sitar music. Their advanced knowledge of harmony—the crowning glory of European

Will Schmid is professor of music at the University of Wisconsin–Milwaukee.

music—does not serve them well when dealing with the music of Japan where heterophony is the prime vertical element. Another illustration of this dilemma is the true story of the third-grade music teacher who had just finished singing a folk song with her class, when a student stood up and said, "My uncle doesn't sing it that way, he sings it like this," and proceeded to sing an interesting variant of the song. The teacher, trained only in the European classical tradition, then missed the point and responded by saying, "That's fine, but the version in the book is the original—the way it's supposed to be sung." Although our repertoire has greatly expanded, our preservice college curricula have not changed enough to deal with the increased needs of teachers.

If all of these new musical styles are now to be included in the core of music study at all levels, then how do we decide what is good music? One can make a strong case that there is good music—music worthy of study—in all styles and categories. One advantage of such an attitude is that teachers do not "look down their noses" at the music enjoyed by students. For example, the view that there's good music in all styles and categories allows teachers to see that rap is related to a long tradition that includes talking blues and the story-songs accompanied by mbira from Zimbabwe. Seeing rap (arguably one of the least popular styles among music teachers) in this context might make some of its forms an acceptable part of the curriculum rather than taking the stance that all rap is bad music or not music at all.

One of the most enjoyable classes I ever attended at the Eastman School was a *collegium musicum* on the piano music of Schubert. The professor began with twenty minutes of his worst piano music to make the point that spontaneous composers such as Schubert were bound to write some pretty mediocre stuff that may not deserve a place on "the pedestal." We were rolling in the aisles at how bad it was, and we felt cleansed enough to really appreciate the second half of the presentation, which featured some of his more sublime pieces. The points I

learned that day were that we are not in the business of teaching music "appreciation," but rather music "discrimination," and that good music need not be defended, but rather given a chance through the kind of experience that allows it to work its powers.

In this new world culture with its greatly expanded musical repertoire, our profession needs some new frameworks and vocabulary that will help us process all of this music. Terms such as "rhythm" will continue to serve us well, but other terms or headings will not. A good case in point is the study of "instruments of the orchestra." Although we will continue to value the orchestra and its families of instruments, this unit should become a subset under "musical instruments" and only be considered one of a number of interesting musical ensembles. It is hard to imagine studying the violin without including styles of music such as classical, bluegrass, jazz, South Indian music, Cajun, rock, and swing, but it is done every day when teachers start with the category "Instruments of the Orchestra."

In that spirit, I offer the following outline as some possible ways of dealing with this new diverse repertoire. In most cases the categories of study are not style-specific. They tend to look at music through the natural curiosities that arise in the process of making sense out of what we hear, play, and compose. The outline is not intended to give answers as much as to raise questions and provide some fuel for the dialogue that lies ahead.

Outline for Diverse Repertoire
I. What Is Music?
  A. How are sounds made?
    1. What vibrates/oscillates?
      a) Idiophones, membranophones, chordophones, aerophones, electrophones
      b) Three Ls of musical acoustics
        (1) The longer the lower
        (2) The larger the lower
        (3) The looser the lower

c) Three parts of all instruments
  (1) What starts the tone?
  (2) What vibrates or oscillates?
  (3) What amplifies or resonates?
2. What are instruments made of?
  a) Available materials—plant, animal, mineral (e.g., what is available locally—bamboo, clay, wood?)
  b) If your cow died, what instruments could you make?
3. Instruments and sound producers of various ensembles
  a) Symphony orchestra, rock band, Javanese gamelan, bluegrass band, Dixieland band, chamber groups, contemporary jazz band, Hindustani classical music ensemble, Cajun band, vocal groups of all sorts, and so on
B. Who makes music?
  1. The musical triangle
    a) Creators (composers, improvisers, arrangers, recording engineers)
    b) Performers (conductors, singers, instrumentalists, technicians)
    c) Responders (listeners, movers, dancers)
  2. The music makers—focus on individuals and their roles
    a) Study the lives of famous music makers and how they live and do their art
C. The process—oral and written traditions
  1. Oral/aural music traditions
    a) Navajo ceremonial songs—dreams and visions
    b) Training of a sitar or tabla player from India
    c) Folk music variants (how songs change through the oral tradition)
    d) Improvisation in rock, jazz, and world music traditions
  2. The written score
    a) Manuscript and typescript
    b) MIDI computer-generated music notation: how it is done today
      (1) Sequencers: combining improvisation with recording studio technology
      (2) Music notation programs
  3. Multimedia
D. Elements of music—what terms to use?
  1. Rhythm—the time dimension
    a) Meter
    b) Duration
  2. Melody—the horizontal dimension
    a) Keys and tonal centers
    b) Scales and modes
    c) Phrases
    d) Melodic contour and expression
  3. Harmony—the vertical dimension
    a) Monophony
    b) Heterophony
    c) Polyphony (e.g., drones, parallels, counterpoint)
    d) Intervals and chords
II. How Do We Use Music?
  A. Music in a world perspective
    1. What is a good tone quality?
      a) "Buzzy" sound of Sub-Sahara Africa, African American, and rock
      b) "Clear" bell-like tone of European music
      c) "Nasal" sound of Japanese music and country music
      d) Vibrato, embellishment, and other factors: how do they influence what we like or dislike (e.g., vibrato in operatic singing)
      e) Instruments that sound like the human voice—which came first?
  B. Why do I like/dislike music?
    1. Consonance/dissonance
    2. Repeated experience and how it changes us
  C. How does music function in people's lives?
    1. Work (Is muzak "work" music?)
    2. Social institutions
    3. Beliefs and religious use
    4. Aesthetics
    5. Language
III. How Is Music Organized?
  A. Unity and variety—basic human needs and their expression in music and the arts

1. No-fault improvisation—group performance and decision making
   a) The junk gamelan—"found sound" with hanging percussion
   b) Air for balloon—making music together with balloons
B. How unity is achieved
   1. Steady beat or no beat?
   2. How does an ensemble stay together?
      a) Conductor
      b) Leader within ensemble
      c) Watching, movement, and so on
   3. Repetition—when does too much turn to boredom?
      a) American Indian singing and drumming—the power of repetition
      b) Repetition in rock—extensions of African music
      c) European classical music—Beethoven vs. Tchaikovsky
      d) Minimalism
C. Musical patterns that unify
   1. Motives (also known as "licks")
      a) Beethoven, jazz, Hindustani classical sitar music
   2. Ostinatos and drones
      a) Drones—bagpipes, banjos, tambouras, pedal points, Appalachian dulcimers
      b) Boogie-woogie and twelve-bar blues
      c) Accompaniment arpeggios
      d) Passacaglia and chaconne
   3. Cycles
      a) Song cycles (from Schubert to the Beatles' Abbey Road, side 2, band 3)
      b) Bell (gong) cycles (from Africa to Indonesia)
      c) Tala in the music of India
   4. The return of A
      a) AABA 32-bar song form
      b) Rondo—ABA, ABABA, ABACA, ABACABA
D. How variety is achieved
   1. Changing the basic elements
   2. Theme and variations
      a) European classical compositions
      b) Koto pieces from Japan
      c) Dixieland and jazz variations
   3. Singing with variation
      a) Ballads—folk and pop
      b) The da capo aria
   4. Improvisation—soloing over a basic structure
      a) Jazz and rock solos
      b) African drumming
      c) Bluegrass fiddle tunes
   5. Sonata-allegro form
   6. Different settings of the same music
   7. Larger extended forms

Peter Webster explores the links between projections about schools of the future and music educators' growing interests in musical thinking and musical processes. Music education that focuses on creativity and imagination, composition, and improvisation is congruent with schools that emphasize student-centered learning, group problem solving, individual decision making, new forms of assessment, development of thinking skills, and time for reflection. Citing experiences of students in a middle school general music class and examples of software, Webster illustrates the role of technology in the schools and general music classes of the future.

General Music, School Reform, and Technology

By Peter Webster

The conventional "technology" of the classroom is a thousand-year-old invention initially adopted to discipline an esoteric cadre of ascetic monks. The institution of contemporary, public education is a nineteenth-century innovation designed as a worker-factory for an industrial economy. Both have as much utility in today's modern economy of advanced information technology as the Conestoga wagon or the blacksmith shop. (Perelman, 1992)

Most of the children born in 1994 will end first grade in the twenty-first century. What will schools be like for these children as the new century unfolds? What will music education be like? These questions and others like them occupy the thinking of music educators and those who prepare them. This symposium may help to answer some of these questions, and those organizing this event are to be congratulated for their efforts. We need to do this more frequently.

Some answers are already clear. When the music education historians of the future characterize the closing of the twentieth century, they will undoubtedly speak of the interest shown in

Peter Webster is professor of music education in the School of Music, Northwestern University, Evanston, Illinois.

musical thinking. They will note the move from focus on the *products* of music performance to a more comprehensive concern with the *processes* associated with music composition, improvisation, music listening, and performance. They will note this trend beginning in the sixties, seventies, and eighties with curriculum experiments such as the Manhattanville Project and the Contemporary Music Project (CMP) and with symposia such as Tanglewood, Yale, and Ann Arbor. The nineties will be remembered for the rise of affordable technology to assist this focus on musical thinking and the establishment of new professional standards of excellence from MENC and other arts education associations that formed the foundation for these changes.

School Reform Issues That Affect Us All

Of course, none of this happens in a vacuum. The signs of this focus on thinking and on process are present in all of education as the century closes. A review of the many books and articles written on school reform point to at least five issues that are key for education and for music education specifically:

■ Project-centered learning with group problem solving

■ Student-centered learning and decision making

- Critical and creative thinking
- Time for imagination and reflection
- Personal record keeping as a way to "own" one's education

These ideas are treated at length by Gardner (1991) and Papert (1993) in recent books on school reform that I highly recommend. I will describe each key idea briefly and relate these to one teacher's general music class. This will lead to some examples of music software that offer especially good support for these ideas.

Project-Centered Learning with Group Problem Solving. Individual learning is very important in all school disciplines, but should this always be done in isolation or as a competitive race between individuals? Many educators believe that the kind of learning that accrues from group work is essential to developing solid thinking skills and makes independent work easier. Children often learn more from each other when they work together with the teacher, rather than as individuals working only with teacher feedback. Some combination of group and individual work is more consistent with real-world achievement, and much can be learned about life and people using such arrangements. Many feel that school learning ought to center around projects and problem solving. Imagine how this might work in music as children discuss together solutions for listening problems or composition tasks (Wiggins, 1989).

Student-Centered Learning with Decision Making. Gone are the days when the teacher knows all and the students know nothing. That model was appropriate when education was conducted using an industrial-age model, but that is hardly the case now as we enter the next century. The rising amount of information and experience that each child brings to school from his or her own environment is enormous. Much of this information and experience is rich with implications for schooling as we encourage children to learn to think and work with others. Children need to learn to make decisions on their own and be allowed to fail occasionally. Part of learning to think effectively is the ability to think for oneself and to make judgments.

Teachers can no longer expect to dominate and direct all learning and to make all of the decisions for their pupils. The teacher, however, *is* an expert on many subjects and is the only one in a position to structure the learning experience for each individual in his or her charge. The key is to make the school experience a shared learning adventure, with each person contributing to his or her own education and to that of others. Imagine a general music classroom where teachers use the genuine music experiences of each child gained at home, at concerts, or on the school playground in order to teach the subtleties of rhythm and melody. Imagine a classroom (or rehearsal for that matter) where children get to make some aesthetic decisions (Davidson, 1990).

Critical and Creative Thinking. School should be more than memorizing facts for a test, more than learning how to manipulate a pencil, computer, or musical instrument for an extrinsic reward. Schools *are* about these things, but it is most important that schools teach the ability to use these lower-level skills for higher-level achievement. Schools should be about thinking imaginatively and realistically, about divergent and convergent thinking (Webster & Richardson, 1993). Children need to learn to apply facts and skills in interesting and meaningful ways. If this is done well, school can be an exciting and fun place. Imagine a general music class where children create, perform, listen, and critically think about music of their own and others all the time.

Time for Imagination and Reflection. In order for such thinking to occur, children need time to imagine and reflect—time that is rare in today's fast-paced, packed curriculum. Perhaps it is time to slow things down, to take a little longer to linger over ideas, to play a little. Is it necessary to learn so many facts, to acquire so many skills? Perhaps it is time to change our values about quantity and take a hard look at quality. In early grades, we often encourage imaginative stories and images, ask "what if" questions, and give children some "quiet time." As children get older, this becomes less important because they need to behave more like adults. Knowledge necessary to pass standardized tests seems to be more important than learning how to think about content. Imagine music classes where children are asked to "think in sound" by composing or improvising (Webster, 1990).

Personal Record Keeping as a Way to "Own" One's Education. This idea speaks to a fundamental change in the way schools deal with assessment. Assessment of children is opened to include not only the professional evaluation by the teacher, but also the child's own view. This approach encourages children to take ownership of their own learning. If creative, project-centered work is employed, the objects of assessment themselves are also broadened to include more than just test scores. Other monuments of higher-level thinking are included and are subject to analysis. By studying these portfolios of student work collectively over time, teachers and parents, as well as students themselves, can view progress. Diagnostic recommendations are not handed down from on high in a mysterious way, but rather as part of a team approach that is open to all. Imagine general music teachers who assess genuine musical growth on more than trivial tests and subjective personal reactions (Wolf, 1988).

A Real Example

One example of a teaching approach in music that embraces many of these ideas can be noted in the work of Tammy Greshiw-Nardi, a junior high school general music specialist in Park Ridge, Illinois. She offers an elective music composition class for eighth-grade students. The class is organized around a set of composition projects that are completed by students in small groups of three or four. The students must create short compositions, but they do so cooperatively. The teacher offers structure for each project by providing a set of problems to solve and suggestions for how to proceed. Models are given by playing projects from past student work. Inexpensive computers and synthesizers on carts are used to form portable workstations.

After meeting as a full class, students push the carts into practice rooms and work in groups with the equipment. Greshiw-Nardi moves from room to room, offering help and suggestions as needed. Students are encouraged to create their own solutions, exercising their own creative and critical thinking.

One project, for instance, asks that each group create a rap song. Students are asked to divide up the work with one student working on the lyrics, another the bass line and drum patterns, and another on the keyboard fills. This is only a suggestion, however, and other ways of cooperatively working on the project are also possible. Students are not expected to complete the assignment immediately, but rather to work on it over a few weeks. Reflection and revision is encouraged. The final version is captured on tape for listening later on, and each student receives his or her own copy to share with others. Group projects are used in class as the basis for detailed discussions about music. The work becomes part of a portfolio of these and other achievements that serve as the basis for the teacher's grade. Greshiw-Nardi's class meets each quarter and is fully subscribed each time it is offered.

Role of Technology

Greshiw-Nardi's class uses technology in its work because of the flexible support that sequencing and notation software offer composition projects. Clearly, the teacher's goals could be accomplished without the use of computers and synthesizers, but having such tools allows students to realize their musical ideas quickly and powerfully. They can hear their ideas, alter them, and save the results for another day. Such music technology allows the application of many of the school reform ideas noted above.

Sequencing and notation titles are not the only types of software technology that might be used. Traditional drill and practice software (based on older models of the "teacher-knows-all" philosophy) has given way to a flexible practice category that takes advantage of new technology and the new ideas associated with school reform. Key features for flexible practice include:

- Comprehensive approach with multiple tasks
- Intelligent branching tailored to individual need
- Realistic music examples within a musical context
- Flexibility for student and teacher in designing learning environments
- On-line tutoring for music concepts.

In addition to flexible practice, other categories of music software design have emerged in recent times that offer a whole new way to think about music teaching with technology. Two of these are based directly on music teaching and learning goals, namely "simulation" and "multimedia."

Simulation software provides the student with a chance to practice music decision making in real-world music settings. Rather than focusing on specific skill development in the form of drills that often reduce the music experience to an atomistic and unmusical level, simulation software takes a more holistic approach. It provides the individual an opportunity to interact with the technology system in a way that is as similar as possible to the four ways humans create music experiences: listening, performing, composing, and improvising. Depending on which of these experiences is being stressed, key characteristics typically include:

- Interactive platforms for manipulation of aural and visual images
- MIDI sound sources, with frequent use of a MIDI instrument as an input device
- Emulation of real-world music experiences with freedom to experiment with aesthetic choices
- Frameworks in which the

student has creative control.

Multimedia computer software is a unique merger of learning resources. Text information can be augmented with a number of graphics, including line drawings, still pictures, graphic animation, and slow-motion or real-time video. This alone provides a powerful set of learning tools for teaching about the subtleties of music, but that's only the beginning. The highest quality sound can be added to this mix, usually with the use of audio compact discs that can be asked to play music excerpts ranging from a fraction of a second to the entire disc! Internal sound within the computer is also possible of course, along with attached MIDI instruments. All of this combines to offer an unusually powerful and flexible environment for teaching about music. Key characteristics typically include:

- Nonlinear exploration by the teacher and student
- Accommodation for different learning styles
- Multiple aural and visual resources used for specific learning objectives
- Manipulation of imagery.

Figure 1 graphically portrays these newer cat-

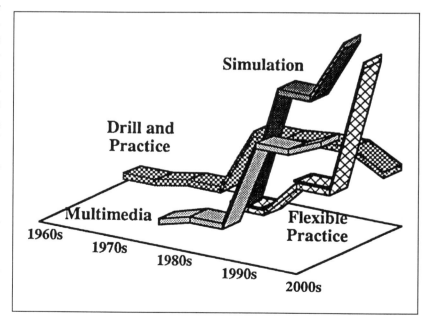

Figure 1. Music teaching software categories.

egories with more traditional skill building software in terms of importance for the future. Note the continued rise of flexible practice, simulation, and multimedia into the next millennium. (Williams & Webster, in press).

Software Examples

Here are some examples of music teaching software that dramatically supports the emerging ideas on school reform. Using the newer categories of simulation and multimedia, I have chosen teaching software for composition,

Figure 2. Music Mania.

improvisation, and music listening. Each is designed to work with general music students who have no previous music experience. Each encourages creative and critical thinking in either groups or in individual settings. Each allows children to make aesthetic decisions and save those products for further reflection or as final products.

Composition. Music Mania is custom-design HyperCard stack developed at Northwestern University (Hickey, 1993). The program is designed to lead elementary-aged school children through a series of exploratory experiences with melody, rhythm, harmony/texture, timbre, and form. The children explore these elements by creating music on an attached MIDI synthesizer, and the program saves their explorations. Figure 2 displays a screen that comes at the end of the experimentation with, in this case, melody. Notice that the children can (a) go to the "Recording Studio" to complete tasks that verify their understanding of melody, (b) click on "Scrapbook" to save their favorite melodies to use later, or (c) go to "Reflections," which allows them to write about their experiences or their music. A final project at the end of all this exploration encourages the children to combine the elements to form a composition by creating

new music or by using favorite scrapbook elements. The program never models actual music, but rather gives children conceptual information that motivates them to make aesthetic decisions. All the compositions that the children complete are saved for later analysis by the teacher or researcher.

Improvisation. Music Mouse (Spiegel, 1989) is a program designed for those interested in exploring sound with improvisation. The computer becomes a music instrument of sorts with the mouse controlling harmony and melody and the typewriter keyboard offering controls for changing musical properties. As figure 3 demonstrates, the intersection of the vertical and horizontal lines is controlled by the mouse and results in the changing of pitch for both harmony and melody. Keyboard controls specify volume, scale types (such as major, minor, pentatonic, and chromatic), style (legato or staccato), and other musical parameters. The sound can be realized by a MIDI device or by digitized sound from the computer. The software can be used by general music teachers to encourage children to play with sound and for children to create intricate, improvised compositions without needing extensive psychomotor skills.

Listening. Again using the power of the com-

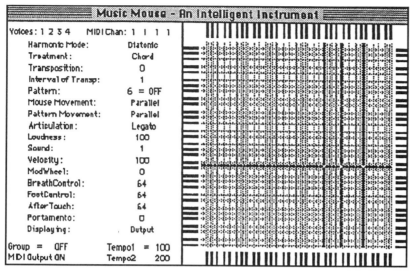

Figure 3. Music Mouse.

puter and an attached MIDI sound device, the author of the program in figure 4 has chosen to offer the listener an opportunity to "mess" with the first movement of Mozart's famous serenade, *Eine Kleine Nachtmusik* (Reese, 1993). Here the focus is on rhythm as the child can change tempo, rhythm patterns, and meter to hear the changes in musical quality. The original version is always available to listen to for comparison. Similar "what if" experiments are supported in chapters on timbre, melody, harmony, and form. Because of the technology, a listener can change the orchestration, melodic contour, complexity of the harmony, and even the order of the musical phrases. These experiences allow the listener to increase understanding about the complexities of musical structure and the affective response that comes with it. Regardless of whether the listener is beginning to explore the music, reflecting on its overall effect, or constructing a full mental analysis, the technology provides useful support.

Music Education in the Next Century

I have tried to offer a few answers to my opening questions of what schools and music education will be like in the next century. It is my hope that school will be a far different place than it is today. If we do our jobs well, children ought to be excited about learning and thinking. Music education will have a far broader mission, touching a far wider audience with many musical experiences. My guess is that technology will play a major role in making this happen. Although admittedly somewhat radical, Lewis Perelman's words in the opening quotation are worth reading again.

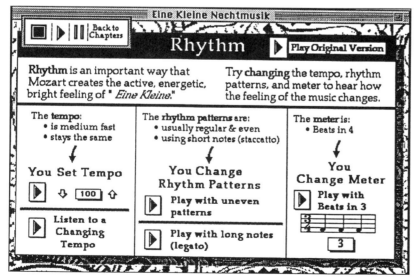

Figure 4. Eine Kleine Nachtmusik.

References

Davidson, L. 1990. Tools and environments for musical creativity. *Music Educators Journal* 76, No. 9: 47–51.

Gardner, H. 1991. *The unschooled mind: How children think and how schools should teach.* New York: Basic Books.

Hickey, M. 1993. *Music mania* [computer program]. School of Music, Northwestern University. (Contact Maud Hickey, School of Music, Ithaca College, Ithaca, New York.)

Papert, S. 1993. *The children's machine: Rethinking school in the age of the computer.* New York: Basic Books.

Perelman, L. 1992. *School's out: The new hyperlearning, technology, and the end of education.* New York: Morrow.

Reese, S. 1993. *Eine Kleine Nachtmusik.* [computer program]. Champaign, IL: Electronic Courseware Systems.

Spiegel, L. 1989. *Music mouse.* [computer program]. Needham, MA: Dr. T's Music Software.

Webster, P. & Richardson, C. 1993. Asking children to think about music. *Arts Education Policy Review* 94, No. 3: 7–11.

Webster, P. 1990. Creativity as creative thinking. *Music Educators Journal* 76, No. 9: 22–28

Wiggins, J. 1989. Composition as a teaching tool. *Music Educators Journal* 75, No. 8: 35–38.

Williams, D. & Webster, P. In press. *Computers, technology, and the music experience.* New York: Schirmer Books.

Wolf, D. 1988. Opening up assessment. *Educational Leadership* 45, No. 4: 24–29.

Integrating technology into the general music curriculum, states Jacqueline H. Wiggins, allows students to use "tools of their own culture" to develop understanding about all kinds of music. Key to effective integration is an emphasis on problem-solving approaches that nurture independence in music making and musical thinking, as well as a highly interactive learning environment. Wiggins cites examples from her own teaching to illustrate the uses of technology in the classroom and the role of technology in the general music curriculum.

Where Does Technology Belong in the General Music Curriculum?

By Jacqueline H. Wiggins

Music produced through electronic media occupies a central place in the cultural lives of the children we teach. For the most part, music as our students know it—whether it is on television, from CDs, or in movies—has been composed, performed, altered, edited, and recorded through digital technology. As musicians and music teachers, have we given due recognition to this phenomenon? From our position as experts in the field of music, our credibility—our expertise in what music *is* in the eyes of our students—is at stake.

Including technology in the classroom curriculum and acknowledging its importance in the lives of the students we teach can extend our credibility to all other aspects of the music program, not only in the eyes of our students, but also in the eyes of our colleagues, administrators, parents, and the community at large. The issue is one of relevance, of credibility, of motivation, and of the importance of what we do in the eyes of the children we teach. It involves their perception of school music as real music.

Lots of attention is being paid today to the importance of recognizing cultural diversity in the classroom. In some ways, the broadest cultural gap in the music classroom is between the teacher and the students. The majority of the students we teach, regardless of cultural heritage, shares a common bond in their understanding and knowledge of the pop culture, which is usually expressed in digital technology. Synthesizers and computers are truly the tools of our children's musical culture.

We need to allow children to develop as musicians in a setting that recognizes their own musical culture. "School music" and "real music" cannot be viewed by children as two separate entities in their lives. The music classroom takes on a whole new image when children are given an opportunity to work with sounds with which they are familiar and when they are allowed to work within stylistically familiar genres. Electronic media need only occupy one small place in the curriculum for its presence to be felt throughout that curriculum. By integrating technology into a curriculum designed to teach about all music, students are given the opportunity to use the tools of their own culture to manipulate and develop an understanding of the structural aspects common to all music. When they are allowed to learn in this fashion, they can begin with the familiar and then gradually widen their circle of understanding of music

Jacqueline H. Wiggins is assistant professor of music education at Oakland University in Rochester, Michigan.

and begin to accept and understand all styles and forms of music.

Many music teachers do recognize the importance of this perspective and would like to get involved in using the new technology in their classrooms. Many of them, however, are a bit fearful of having to use with youngsters equipment that they have only just begun to know how to use themselves. I believe that the fears of music teachers go beyond their concerns about using the equipment. Musicians have fears about what they perceive to be an electronic revolution that may be leaving us, as a profession, behind. For many of us, these fears are rooted in our perceptions of this revolution as a threat to musical production as we know it. We worry about the potential of this new technology to replace traditional composition and performance practice. We worry about the threat these media seem to pose to the future of both Western art music and the traditional folk music of the cultures of the world. We worry about the fact that our own backgrounds may not have included learning about electronic media, and that the musical skills and knowledge we value may become obsolete in this rapidly changing world.

In addition to our fears about the future of music as we know it and about our own lack of knowledge about the media, music educators who do take the time to seek out some of the technological programs available to schools often develop an additional concern. Many of the programs and equipment available today are being marketed as whole curriculum packages, designed to replace existing curricula. Of those that are not, many deal with areas that are not really in the realm of what we believe to be important in a general music curriculum.

Taking all of this into account, it is not difficult for music teachers to develop a view that bringing technological equipment into the classroom means: (1) giving up the study of the kinds of music we believe to be important in the education of children, (2) sacrificing the curriculum we believe to be important in the education of children, and (3) giving up the security of familiarity and delving into an area that is basically an unknown to us.

I hope that the ideas presented here will allay some of these fears. It is possible to develop an instructional approach that utilizes the wonderful capabilities of technological advances in musical production without sacrificing what we believe to be important in the music education of children. It is also possible for the new digital technology to exist side by side with the more traditional forms of acoustic musical production. It is possible to utilize both electronic and acoustic production media to help students to develop a structural understanding of music of all genres and cultures.

What I am suggesting is integration of technology into the general music classroom to enhance an existing instructional approach. However, not all instructional approaches would lend themselves to the integration of electronic media. Therefore, we are faced with a bit of a dilemma. Do we alter an instructional approach simply to enable us to bring technology into the classroom? Do we ignore electronic media simply because we are not sure how they fit with our instructional approaches? Or is it, perhaps, time for us to look at and reevaluate what we are doing in our classrooms regardless of the integration of technology?

The Importance of Problem Solving

Technology does fit very easily into an instructional approach in which students are actively involved in interactive problem-solving situations. Experts on learning theory agree that problem solving is one of the most effective tools for learning in that it necessitates application of conceptual knowledge to a practical situation.[1] As such, it nurtures, clarifies, and reinforces that conceptual knowledge in the learner. If problem solving is such an important aspect of learning, we need to take a good look at the general music approaches currently in use in our nation's classrooms. Few of them lend themselves to developing true problem-solving situations in which our students can be intellectually engaged with the structural aspects of music and thereby truly come to understand what it is all about.

Most general music teachers today use a variety of activities in their instructional approaches; however, few of the activities most often found in these classrooms include opportunities for independent problem solving. Often, general music education seems to consist of a series of activities in which the teacher knows the purpose, but the students are not necessarily privy to it. Particularly on the elementary level, many of the activities are based on student imitation of a teacher model. Many teachers follow lesson plans that flow from one activity to another, in which the children are led by the teacher, but the children do not necessarily know what they are supposed to be learning. There is an assumption that if the children can do the particular activity that they understand the musical idea behind it when, in reality, they may be imitating or taking cues from the teacher. In well-designed curricula of this nature, the activities do become successively more complex, but the children are often still getting their cues from the teacher, generally through imitation. Children learn to play more and more complex rhythm patterns by chanting in imitation, or by reading some form of notation, but they are not necessarily given the opportunity to gain or demonstrate a true understanding of the principles behind the rhythmic structure of music and the relationship of that rhythmic structure to musical works. Our existing approaches do not seem to nurture independence of the learner. Students are not usually asked to verbalize their understanding or to apply it to other situations on their own or with peers without teacher guidance. The children can make music, but are generally dependent upon the teacher's leadership to do so.

The interactive problem-solving approach I am going to discuss today could be carried out with or without the aid of the new technology. Indeed, I worked from this perspective for many years before getting involved in electronic equipment. From my experience, however, I have found that this particular instructional approach is more effective and more successful with the aid of the new technology because of the high level of student motivation and the fact that the students have so many more possibilities available to them. But let us keep in mind that it is the kind of instructional approach that makes the crucial difference in the nature of the musical learning that takes place in a classroom more than it is the instructional equipment and materials available.

An Interactive Learning Environment

Based on the work of music cognition experts, a general music classroom that is truly an interactive learning environment should provide opportunities for the students to interact with music first hand through performing, creating, and analytical listening.[2] Ideally, these experiences should be interrelated. For example, creative activities should draw upon the understanding that is developed through performing and analytical listening experiences and, of course, performing and listening are integral parts of the creative process.

An interactive learning environment also needs to take into account the role of social interaction in the learning process. Social constructivist learning theorists have emphasized the importance of social interaction in learning.[3] In this view, learning is seen as a social process that occurs first between people and later independently, where the individual utilizes processes learned previously in interaction with others. In the classroom, social interaction includes student–teacher interaction, but also interaction with peers. It is through this interaction with teacher and peers as well as interaction with music that musical learning occurs in a classroom.

Technology in an Interactive Learning Environment

Now, what might an interactive learning environment that includes digital equipment look like? In the situation where I work, I have not had access to computers for my students, so what I will share is some of what I have done with synthesizers in a general music classroom over the past ten years. A synthesizer is an instrument for making music and a tool for learning about music, but not a music curriculum in and of itself. Therefore, my curriculum does not necessarily reflect the fact that I use these instruments as an instructional tool. The curriculum is designed to enhance the children's understanding of the structural aspects of music through performance, analytical listening, and the creative processes of improvisation and composition. Synthesizers are one option available to the students as they work to solve musical problems. The bulk of the work done by the students in my classes involves some sort of problem solving, that is, performance problems, analytical listening problems, and creative problems.

Problem solving in performance can include projects where the students determine a chord progression that can best accompany a song or where students develop an arrangement of a song, teach one another the parts they have created, rehearse the song on their own, and then perform it for their peers. Problem solving in analytical listening can include analysis of the formal or textural structure of a work or stylistic comparison of a variety of settings of a particular work. Creative problem solving can be an effective instructional and assessment tool in that students can be asked to create an original work that reflects their understanding of a particular listening assignment. The children might look at what professional composers do to handle a certain compositional problem and, with that understanding, set out to create their own solutions to the problem. This can be as simple as creating a piece that uses dynamic changes to create a desired effect, or something more complex such as asking students to create their own variations on a theme after analyzing a piece that utilizes the technique of theme and variation.

In my classroom, some of the problem-solving work is carried out in a whole-class setting, but much of it involves small-group and independent work. Using a variety of instructional settings allows ample opportunity for peer

interaction as well as student–teacher interaction on both formal and informal levels. When working in this manner, opportunities naturally arise for peer teaching and for student–teacher interaction of an apprenticeship nature. It is also important to recognize that for students to develop musical independence, they must be involved in musical activities that are not teacher directed. Teachers must be willing and able to step down from the front of the room and allow the students to take the initiative to find out more about how music works on their own. Electronic instruments can play a key role in a classroom that allows for a variety of instructional strategies and formats.

In developing problem-solving situations for students, it is important to recognize that the structural elements of which music is made do not exist in isolation. Music is never *only* loud or *only* fast. It is more than just rhythm and pitch. The effect of a whole musical work is dependent on the ways in which all of the elements of music interact within that whole. To teach musical elements in isolation is to teach them out of context. Further, to teach musical elements with no music present is not teaching music at all. Studying tempo or dynamics in a nonmusical setting is not studying music. It is essential that the material for all music lessons be drawn from and relate back to a whole musical work, be it a piece for listening, a song for singing or a piece to be created. When extracting a particular musical element for study, it is essential that the children understand the relationship between that element and the musical work from which it is drawn. It is not enough for the teacher to have that knowledge. The children need to have knowledge of the musical context from which the particular musical elements are drawn and of their function within that context. Contextual understanding is crucial to conceptual understanding.

It is through direct interaction with music that students develop musicianship and musicality. In general music classrooms, it often seems that the most prevalent form of musical interaction is performing under teacher direction. As students get older, teacher-guided listening lessons tend to become more prominent. In general, it seems that music teachers tend to shy away from genuine creative activities. Few seem to include student composition or improvisation as integral components of their classroom activities. Most of us would think it problematic if we were told of a language curriculum in which children read and were read to, but never engaged in writing experiences. There is an expectation in the teaching of language (be it one's own or a foreign language) that children need to speak, hear, read, and write language in order to become fully competent. Yet many of us assume that children can become competent musicians without ever encountering the opportunity to manipulate music with their own hands. The creating of music is not only for the gifted few. Composing and improvising are musical processes that are essential to the development of musical understanding.

Within a general music program such as the one described here, the children basically use synthesizers as media for performance and composition. As they perform, compose, improvise, or work to solve musical problems, synthesizers should be only one option available. They should be used in conjunction with a selection of acoustic classroom instruments and the children should generally have free choice of media in creative activities. Admittedly, the electronic instruments are often the most popular option and most interesting to the children. In both my research and classroom experience, however, I have found that children presented with the option of choosing either electronic or acoustic instruments seem to make the choice with a great deal of consideration and sensitivity. It is not uncommon for a group of children to begin a project at a keyboard or drum synthesizer only to abandon it in search of an acoustic sound that more clearly matches the timbre they seek.

Musicians who are concerned about the future of acoustic musical production need only to observe children at work, and their fears would be allayed. Children may be fascinated by a drum synthesizer and revel in its capabilities

and possibilities, but they also revel in beating a wonderful acoustic drum. On more than one occasion, I have observed students work to create a drum track, but once it is created, tire of pushing the play button and listening to the machine playing their music for them. Sometimes these children then opt for live performance on the drum machine instead. Still others abandon the machine altogether and wander off in search of acoustic percussion instruments to recreate the same pattern in live performance.

They also have no qualms about combining acoustic and electronic instruments in one composition. Students often opt to use acoustic drums, for example, or a lovely little glockenspiel in combination with electronic sounds. Some students will create an acoustic piece and include one or two electronic sound effects to embellish their work. The opportunity to experience both acoustic and electronic media helps children to develop stylistic judgment. They learn to weigh the criteria and select what they believe to be a more appropriate vehicle for the sounds they want to produce.

In selecting instruments, consider choosing instruments that have the capability of making beautiful as well as unusual musical sounds, and the capability of responding to the musical expressiveness of the children. It is important that the instruments enable the children to use them as a vehicle for expression. Professional-calibre synthesizers offer students a wide palette of sounds from which to draw and many options for a variety of expressive qualities.

Using technology as a teaching tool does not mean giving up the study of the kinds of music or curricula we believe to be important in the education of children. While using new equipment does mean that music teachers will need to further educate themselves and will also need to take a good look at the kinds of teaching they are doing in their classrooms, it is hard to consider the need for professional growth as problematic to the profession. Rather we need to accept it as a wonderfully exciting challenge.

It is not really a difficult challenge. The

equipment involved in music technology has become more and more user-friendly so that teachers and students can become quite proficient within a very short period of time. Because of their versatility, synthesizers can be used to accompany many different kinds of songs—even traditional folk songs. Students can listen to an orchestral work, analyze it in terms of specific criteria, and then use synthesizers create an original work that reflects those same criteria. Used in ways such as these, synthesizers can be tools for learning about music of a multitude of styles, historical periods, and cultures. Music teachers actually need a relatively small amount of knowledge about the equipment itself, but a much greater understanding of its place in the music program.

It is easy to find a place for these wonderful instruments in a program that allows time for students to interact with the "stuff music is made of" on their own—involving them in problem-solving situations and hands-on projects. In light of what learning theorists and music cognition experts tell us about ways in which children learn, it is important for our profession to consider adopting a non–teacher-centered, problem-solving approach to musical learning in the general music classroom.

If we present electronic media as an integral part of what music is in our world, the electronic revolution will not leave us behind. We will nurture a generation that perceives electronic

musical production as one option, but a generation that has an understanding of alternative options as well. The instruments themselves really pose no threat to the future of traditional musical production. They possess many exciting capabilities for musical expressiveness, and should be recognized for the potential they offer. As a profession, we must recognize the importance of digital technology in musical production today and learn to make use of its capabilities to bridge the cultural gap between music teachers and students to ensure that learning about music of all kinds will continue to be an important part of the education of our nation's children.

Notes

1. Jerome S. Bruner. *The Process of Education.* (Cambridge: Harvard University Press, 1960).

2. For example, Mary L. Serafine. *Music As Cognition: The Development of Thought in Sound.* (New York: Columbia University Press, 1988); John A. Sloboda, Ed. *Generative Processes in Music.* (Oxford: Clarendon Press, 1988); and Keith Swanwick. *Music, Mind and Education.* (London: Routledge, 1988).

3. Lev Semenovich Vygotsky. *Mind in Society: The Development of Higher Psychological Processes,* edited by M. Cole, V. John-Steiner, S. Scribner, and E. Souberman. (Cambridge: Harvard University Press, 1978).

Daniel M. LeJeune describes a middle school general music class in which students compose musical works using acoustic MIDI technology. Composition activities include both acoustic instruments and electronic technology as means of learning more about music. LeJeune maintains that these experiences engage student creativity and provide a foundation for further musical exploration.

General Music in the Middle School
Developing Student Creativity Using Music and Technology

By Daniel M. LeJeune

In 1992, Chris Patton gave an exciting presentation titled "Sonic Synergy" for our seventh-grade students. Using music technology, Patton devised ways for students to manipulate sounds and create their own music, regardless of ability or previous experience. He showed students how sounds could work together and be changed using technology. More important, he challenged them to become creators of music. The students responded with great enthusiasm because they were directly involved in the process of composing music.

Students in general music classes should be given the chance to invent their own musical material. Lessons in musical composition can be an extension of other musical learning—listening and responding to music, playing instruments, singing, reading, and other activities develop essential musical skills. Engaging in musical composition, however, challenges children to use higher-order thinking skills such as evaluation and synthesis. Musical composition also gives children the satisfaction of creating

music that has personal meaning to them.

Music technology greatly expands the possibilities for developing student creativity in general music. Since its inception in the early 1980s, Musical Instrument Digital Interface (MIDI) has transformed the music industry. By establishing a standard form of communication about music, MIDI makes it possible to create a wide range of music using computers and digital instruments. Through the integration of basic music technology and musical concepts, general music programs have the capability of enhancing musical learning by allowing students to create music with virtually limitless possibilities.

MIDI technology has many advantages. Using a basic computer, software, and synthesizer, students can record, edit, and notate music with ease. In addition to keyboards, there are now wind, guitar, mallet, percussion, and other digital instruments (controllers) that will allow students to enter their music into the computer by playing any one of these instruments. Because digitally recorded music can be played back and edited quickly, a student can repeatedly evaluate his or her work and make modifications. Students who are unable to perform their music easily can change to a more comfortable tempo. This makes it possible for a student of

Daniel M. LeJeune is a general music teacher at Patapsco Middle School, Howard County, Maryland.

any ability to be successful at composing. Once entered, a piece can be played back at any tempo, regardless of how it was originally performed. One additional benefit is that students can wear headphones and record their music without being heard by others. The music can later be retrieved and played back without anyone knowing whose it is, which allows students to be objective when they evaluate the work of their peers.

Linking this technology to musical composition in general music is best done when students create music within a predetermined structure. Having children compose music successfully requires that certain musical variables be controlled. The activity must have a clear focus, otherwise the children will become easily frustrated and overwhelmed by a task that seems impossible. Within a well-defined structure, children will then have freedom to explore their musical ideas.

Students also need to be taken through a sample process of creating music. Providing a model gives them a basis for their own work and lets them know that the task is possible. If students are to take the risk, they must feel comfortable with the task from the very beginning. Once they understand what is expected, they will be more inclined to do their best work.

Scheduling will often determine how much student composition will be taught. In my school, I see students for only nine weeks per year. I use three to four weeks to teach a composition unit, and it is possible for my students to develop and create a musical composition within that time. For now, students use mallet percussion instruments when composing due to a lack of keyboards. Even with the most basic mallet skills, students can compose a wide variety of music. After they have practiced on the acoustic instruments, the students play the music on the digital mallet controller at the MIDI workstation. Students generally find the digital mallet controller as easy to play as the acoustic instrument.

During the initial year of using music technology in my classroom, I piloted several types

of simple composition activities with my students. Three of these activities have worked particularly well. In sixth grade, students composed a pentatonic melody and three accompanying ostinatos. The seventh-grade students composed a calypso melody, and eighth-grade students created a new melody for a piece that uses repeated harmony: Pachelbel's Canon in D.

Sixth graders begin the unit by learning a sixteen-beat rhythmic phrase through body percussion. After orchestrating this rhythm with unpitched percussion instruments, students devise a melody using mallet percussion. The class decides on a melody by taking ideas from various students. We discuss how an accompaniment can be added simply by using three ostinatos: bass, melodic, and unpitched percussion. In order to provide contrasting patterns, students experiment by listening to a pattern played with the melody. Choosing the three best patterns takes time, but the outcome is well worth it. After entering these patterns into the computer sequencer, students are free to orchestrate the song any way they choose using the instrument sounds of the synthesizer. This lets students experiment with a wide variety of tone colors and textures for each part. Once the class has composed, notated, and orchestrated music together, it is much easier for students to work alone or with a partner following the same steps to compose their own original composition.

Seventh-grade students become familiar with calypso music by first listening to an authentic steel band playing calypsos. After discussing the origins of the music, students learn the song "Water Come A Me Eye" from the American edition of *Music for Children*. They immediately respond to the variety of straight and syncopated patterns in the melody and accompaniment ostinatos. After the class has performed the calypso together on pitched and unpitched percussion instruments, they identify melodic, rhythmic, and structural characteristics of the melody, "Water Come A Me Eye." Using this song as a model, students begin to compose their own calypso melody based on its harmonic structure. First, they construct the melodic rhythm based on the patterns they performed in the melody and accompaniment. I show them the places where tonic or dominant chord tones are needed in order to fit the harmony. Once the students have created a melody, they play it at the MIDI workstation. The computer sequencer is programmed to play the accompaniment while the melody is being recorded. Students can immediately hear their work and easily make corrections. For the final step, students notate their melodies and receive a computer-generated copy of their score.

Eighth-grade students use the melody of Pachelbel's Canon in D as a model for composing a new melody to the same harmony of the canon. After students perform the various patterns of the accompaniment on mallet percussion instruments, they analyze the structure and patterns of Pachelbel's melody. Students are asked to describe characteristics of several other examples of Baroque music, art, and architecture. Once they understand the highly ornamented style of the Baroque period, the class develops a harmonic outline for a melody. This outline consists of one chord tone per measure, chosen from the I-V-vi-iii-IV-I-IV-V progression of the piece. The students ornament this outline with harmonic and nonharmonic tones. Each student then follows this same procedure in creating an individual melody. Using the computer sequencer to record the melodies, all students can hear what their new melody sounds like with a full orchestra playing Pachelbel's accompaniment. This allows them to evaluate the quality of their melodies and make changes until they are satisfied.

These examples illustrate only a small fraction of the potential for using music technology in general music. Although music technology cannot entirely replicate the natural sound of acoustic instruments or the nuances of human instrumental and vocal performance, it can offer many tools for teaching children how to organize and express their musical ideas. I hope that these experiences will spark student creativity and provide children with a foundation for continued musical exploration outside of the classroom.

Meaningful integration of music with the other arts and other subjects requires that music educators seek frameworks that preserve the integrity of the aesthetic experience within the context of curricular connections. Carol Scott-Kassner explores the possibilities for curricular integration and presents models for planning and implementing multidisciplinary educational experiences. Working collaboratively and adapting new "lenses," she notes, allows teachers to develop instruction that stimulates "authentic growth" in music as well as other subjects, and helps students connect what is learned to their communities and their world.

Music, the Arts, and Other Subjects
Maintaining Musical Integrity in the Integrated Curriculum

By Carol Scott-Kassner

As the calls for school reform ring in our ears, music educators feel compelled to respond but are often unsure which direction to take. We have struggled long and hard, with varying degrees of success, to have music recognized and accepted as an important discipline worthy of study in its own right. The new *National Standards for Arts Education* should help to place a clear vision of these disciplines on the table of school reform.

Yet, just when a comprehensive and sequential program has been articulated at the national level, we are being asked by fellow educators to break down the boundaries of our discipline and work within broader, interdisciplinary frames. So we feel pulled, perhaps even more so as general music educators, because we have always attempted to connect music to the rest of the world in which our students live. Curriculum integration, particularly at the elementary level, seems appealing and not altogether unfamiliar.

Carol Scott-Kassner is a professor of music education at the University of Central Florida.

We need to be clear, however, about what we may be losing as well as gaining when we agree to work more collaboratively. We also need to be clear about our role in planning as well as in implementing an effective integrated curriculum. Finally, we need to be able to assess whether the outcomes of the programs we have implemented have resulted in authentic growth or simply the superficial.

Heidi Hayes Jacobs (1989), an expert on interdisciplinary curriculum from Columbia University, has summarized the advantages and disadvantages of both the discipline-based and the interdisciplinary approaches: "The advantage of the disciplines is that they permit schools to investigate with systematic attention to the progressive mastery of closely related concepts and patterns of reasoning" (p. 7). In music and the other arts, we also emphasize the progressive mastery of skills of performance and creative expression. Yet, moving throughout the day from one discipline to another with no connections often leaves students with a sense of fragmentation and the idea that what they learn in school is not related to life outside of school.

The interdisciplinary curriculum helps to create greater relevance by consciously applying what Jacobs describes as "methodology and language from more than one discipline to examine a central theme, issue, problem, topic, or experience" (p. 8). An effective interdisciplinary curriculum creates connections while respecting the unique contributions of the disciplines to be combined.

Problems occur when these are not true connections but merely a sampling of knowledge from each discipline. An example in music might be when the music teacher is asked, usually over lunch, to teach a frog song to fit with a first-grade science unit. This reduces music to a peripheral activity, not an integral part of a broader scheme. Learning to sing a song about frogs is not music education. This potpourri problem (Jacobs, 1989) can only be solved through careful discussion and planning by a team of educators. With such planning, the music specialist may find that the first-grade frog unit coincides with work she is doing on pitch motion, including melodic leaps. She also sees ways that working with poetry about frogs would help her further develop planned rhythm work as well as reinforce the concepts of ostinato and motive. As the classroom teachers discuss some of the concepts children will be learning about frogs, the music specialist sees that she could use the stages of the life cycle as a basis for creative movement and composition, further expanding children's awareness of form. Careful planning and communication can enhance curriculum integration and bring greater meaning to all that children do.

Another conflict can occur when polarities arise in the planning process, with people feeling that the choice is either to work within disciplines or across disciplines (Jacobs, 1989). Students need to have varied curriculum experiences reflecting both approaches. Because education in the arts is not just about ideas, it is crucial that sequential training in the arts disciplines be recognized as important and necessary. Because of the sensory, expressive, and integrative power of the arts, however, it is also important they be included in curriculum integration.

Schools wishing to implement an integrated curriculum need to create conditions for success. First, teachers must be given enough time to plan together. Drake (1993) suggests that a period of approximately ten days is an optimum time to build a full unit. These days could be clustered before school starts, or spread throughout the implementation of the unit. This time is crucial for the building of teamwork and trust as well as planning. Second, leadership and team stability need to be developed. Team stability from the perspective of the specialist teacher is often hard to achieve in elementary music settings where specialists travel to more than one school. Third, budgetary support needs to be provided for materials and other resources, including in-service training, field trips, and artists-in-residence.

At the elementary level, music specialists are often the only specialists to represent the arts. As such, they are in a key role to help teachers think about the content of the arts as they plan for units based on curricular integration. The danger of this position is that, understandably, music specialists often have limited knowledge of the content of arts other than music and therefore feel uncomfortable speaking for visual arts, dance, and drama in planning meetings. Those who find themselves in such a position should seek other resource people to advise them in the planning process.

At the same time, regardless of their background in other arts, music educators can serve an important function on planning teams by constantly asking the question, "How is this stimulating artistic growth?" For, just as singing a song is not music education, neither is drawing a picture art education, or staging a play drama education. All teachers involved in planning for integrated curriculum need to keep the question of significance at the forefront of their decision-making process.

At both the elementary and secondary levels, it is important that music and arts specialists are asked to join teams to plan for integrated curriculum. Lack of background or training in the arts for most teachers often leaves them bereft of the understandings necessary to integrate the arts in artistically significant ways. Teachers in other disciplines are usually grateful when such expertise can be provided by trained arts specialists. Arts educators also need to be willing to participate on planning teams and to suspend rigid thinking about the boundaries of their curricula as they entertain the types of outcomes that can only come through curriculum integration.

Many models exist for curriculum integration. Training in how to structure these models is available through a series of videotapes developed by the Association for Supervision and Curriculum Development (1993). Other publications and consultants are also available to help schools plan effectively for curriculum integration.

At the elementary level, teachers at a particular grade level or across grades may plan an integrated unit that might last from one to twelve weeks. At the secondary level, teachers may get together to plan a parallel curriculum, in which they agree to address similar topics at the same time, while remaining in their separate disciplines. An example would be when the history teacher addresses Elizabethan England while the English teacher focuses on Shakespeare. In the parallel model it may not make sense for all disciplines to try to coordinate. Often secondary teachers will join together to plan and team-teach an interdisciplinary humanities or arts course. Some schools organize their entire curriculum around a topic for a day, or for several weeks. A few schools have committed to a concept in which virtually everything they teach is done from an interdisciplinary perspective.

The Henry A. Wolcott School in Connecticut is an example of a whole-school model in which both disciplinary and interdisciplinary opportunities occur on a regular basis. The principal was able to select teachers committed to this model. Music, theatre, art, and dance are taught as dis-

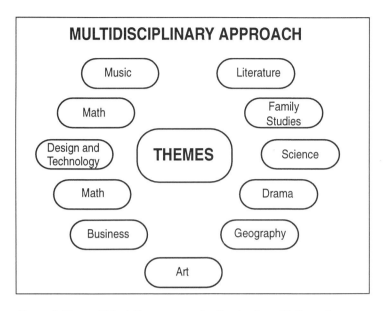

Figure 1. The multidisciplinary approach often begins with thematic or semantic webbing.

ciplines as well as being integrated across the curriculum. Especially exciting are combinations of these with the literary arts.

Perhaps the most common model is the multidisciplinary model (see figure 1). This approach asks: What is important to learn within different disciplines? (Drake, 1993)

Multidisciplinary Approach

Often this approach begins with thematic or semantic webbing, where teachers brainstorm ideas and activities that could be done in various disciplines to focus on the topic. With elementary children, those activities can often be quite basic, yet they contribute to important understandings and skills both within and across disciplines. Understandings often arise as a by-product of the experiences rather than driving the experiences. As teachers work with this model, it is important that they clarify what the likely outcomes are to make sure that they are valuable. Drake (1993) suggests a process of refining the multidisciplinary approach to identify important ideas.

Figure two shows an example of a thematic

web around the topic of rain comes from a book that Patricia Shehan Campbell and I have written.

The ideas in the arts segments of this web were intended to move beyond using the arts as activities to using them to stimulate imagination, aesthetic sensitivity, and critical and creative thinking.

Sometimes the process of planning for themes is much less formal, particularly when it involves arts specialists. Although this is not ideal, it often meets the pragmatic realities of life in schools. Often the general music teacher is given a theme by classroom teachers and asked to reinforce ideas from that theme in the music curriculum. The frog example I gave earlier is illustrative of that process. Another example from one of my recent music education majors is drawn from her willingness to coordinate with a dinosaur unit in the first grades. She agreed to

do a series of musical/artistic activities to reinforce and expand understanding of dinosaurs and help children to grow artistically at the same time. She worked with the classroom teachers to have the children create a mural representing the flora and fauna, as well as the geological surroundings of the age of the dinosaurs. The trees were painted to look as if they were being blown by the wind. Once completed, the mural was mounted on rollers and moved slowly as a changing background to a race by dinosaur-shaped puppets to the music of *William Tell* by Rossini. The music was selected by listening to several different works and judging their appropriateness for this purpose. Through the process, the children not only learned to differentiate between types of dinosaurs and place them in a natural environment, they also developed a sense of forward motion and phrasing in the *William Tell*, which they attempted to show

---

Music
Experiment with rain sounds, using body or instruments as sources. Attempt to convey different kinds of rain. Create a storm. Learn songs about rain. Discuss different qualities. Add rain sounds to accompany. Listen to recorded works about rain. What images are created and how?

Visual Arts
Learn to use various water color techniques, including wash, to create a rain scene. Discuss the way rain mutes the colors of other objects and obscures things outside. Try to reflect that feeling in the painting. Look at the ways other artists create a sense of rain.

Creative Drama
Dramatize settings in which rain, or lack thereof, plays an important role:
■ A young child in a mud puddle
■ A couple, caught in a downpour in the park
■ The first rain after a draught
■ A flood that threatens your property
■ A dog coming in after the rain
Dramatize stories about rain.

Dance
How would you move if you were any of the following:
■ Raindrop
■ Storm
■ Lightning
■ Water down a drain
■ Dripping
Discuss using dance terms. Learn or create a rain dance.

RAIN

Science
Learn about the water cycle. Create one in the classroom. Study what causes rain to fall and which kinds of clouds generate which kinds of rain. Watch the weather report. Interview a reporter—how do they predict.

Mathematics
Construct a rain gauge. Collect and measure rainfall over a period of several weeks. Chart the daily and weekly totals. Compare to monthly report in paper. Research and chart average annual rainfall in your community for the past ten years.

Language Arts
Read various poems about rain. How do the poets create a sense of rain? Do they use onomatopoeia or alliteration? Write your own rain poem using at least five words to describe rain. Read books about rain. How does rain affect people? animals? the environment? Write a story about how rain affects a family.

Social Studies
Look at a map that shows weather patterns. Learn about the lives of people who live with heavy rains, no rains. Learn traditions for asking for rain. Learn the importance of rain to various people.

Figure 2. A thematic web around the topic of rain.

through the artwork and the movement of their puppets.

The multidisciplinary model is often used in exploring the contributions various disciplines can make to the study of other cultures. Music educators have typically contributed to such study by teaching students to perform representative songs, dances, and instrumental works. Although much can be learned through performance, exploring ideas of cultural context, style, transmission, traditions, meaning, and ritual can expand cross-cultural experiences in the arts into much broader interdisciplinary concepts. Students can be encouraged to do ethnographic studies of their own, collecting information on aspects of music from various cultural informants. For example, second graders might interview grandparents to discover their music stories. Grandparents could teach the children favorite songs from their childhood. High school students could interview a professional musician from another culture to elicit answers to questions of training, meaning, and context.

Although interdisciplinary models are normally planned and implemented by a team of teachers, music specialists can readily implement an intersected, or shared, curriculum between music and other art forms within their own classroom. Teachers dedicated to finding ways the arts overlap can do much to reinforce common concepts, heighten aesthetic sensitivity, and stimulate aesthetic development. Perhaps the easiest of the arts to combine are music and dance, since they are both arts of time and their vocabulary is similar. Literary arts and music, as well as dramatic arts and music, also can be combined in a variety of ways. Visual arts and music are more difficult to combine because, though terminology is often similar, the meaning can be very different (for example, texture in visual arts is quite different from texture in music). Many other aesthetically valid

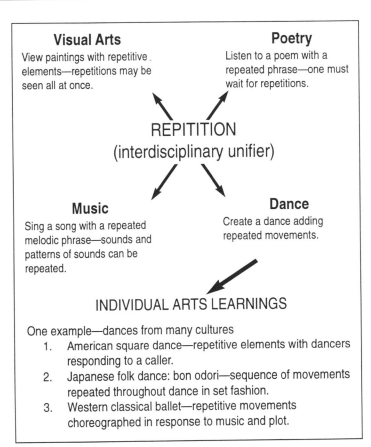

Figure 3. An interdisciplinary model using music and the other art forms, centered around repetition.

connections, however, can be made between music and the visual arts (see figure 3).

Aesthetic principles such as tension and release, repetition and contrast, pattern, line, motive, theme and variation, balance, foreground and background, and density are found in most or all of the arts and are natural ways to view the arts in an interdisciplinary fashion. These broad aesthetic concepts can be introduced in the intermediate grades and expanded through the middle and high school years. Reimer (1989) has suggested an entire curriculum based on this perspective.

Secondary humanities courses that look at broad themes across both Western and non-Western cultures, such as myth, hero, and creation, provide rich possibilities for the arts.

Perkins (1989) argues persuasively for the selection of interdisciplinary themes that have these characteristics: a) are broad and pervasive, b) disclose fundamental patterns, c) reveal similarities and differences, and d) are fascinating to the learner. Possible themes for high school interdisciplinary arts courses might include: creative thinking, aesthetic knowing, media and the arts, or arts and society. Secondary general music teachers can do much to bring creativity and active involvement to interdisciplinary courses in their schools.

Ackerman and Perkins (1989) suggest that teachers weave a metacurriculum of important thinking and learning skills through any interdisciplinary plan. Problem solving, categorizing, sequencing, reading, and writing are some of the skills they suggest. A possible metacurriculum for effective arts integration might be to involve the arts process suggested by Fowler (1976). Fowler highlights six ways in which learners engage in the arts. These processes are all connected and some may occur almost simultaneously. They occur naturally as children construct their world but each can be enhanced through education:

1. Perceiving: taking in information, discerning, being aware of their own art works and the art of others

2. Responding: this could be internal and private or overtly expressed (it could involve feelings, ideas, or actions)

3. Understanding: comprehension of the elements of various arts, the ways arts are produced, the roles the arts play, and the history and sociology of the arts

4. Creating: the process of using the imagination, understandings, and skills to express unique ideas in music (this might take the form of improvisation or composition)

5. Evaluating: the development, refinement, and application of criteria for judging the quality of their own work and the work of others

6. Developing Skills: learning to use the tools, techniques, and elements of various art forms to express ideas.

Keeping elements of this process in mind when developing programs that integrate the arts may help teachers to better answer the question, "How is this stimulating artistic growth?"

Once the planning process has occurred, music educators need to be involved in implementing what they have planned. Their roles can vary from direct teaching, either alone or as part of a team, to guest presenter, to resource person, or consultant/guide.

Finally, all who are involved in implementing the interdisciplinary curriculum need to help establish means of assessing student outcomes in ways authentic to the disciplines and types of outcomes involved. Herman, et. al. (1992) have suggested a variety of means to assess growth in situations that are project- and team-oriented. Questions of content mastery and performance often involve a subjective component, but with careful thought and planning, can be measured reliably.

Integrating the arts throughout the curriculum has the potential for enriching the lives of children and teachers. To be surrounded by and immersed in the arts is to live more fully and more beautifully. If more classrooms and schools did this well, they might become like the country of Bali, where they say, "We have no art; we do everything as well as we can."

References

Ackerman, David and D.N. Perkins. 1989. "Integrating Thinking and Learning Skills across The Curriculum." Chapter 7 of *Interdisciplinary Curriculum: Design and Implementation*. Alexandria: ASCD.

Association for Supervision and Curriculum Development. 1993. *Integrating the Curriculum*, a videotape series for training teachers. Alexandria: ASCD.

Campbell, Patricia Shehan and Carol Scott-Kassner. 1995. *Music in Childhood: From Preschool through the Elementary Years*. NY: Schirmer.

Drake, Susan M. *Planning the Integrated Curriculum: 1993. The Call to Adventure*. Alexandria: ASCD.

Fowler, Charles. 1974. *The Arts Process in Basic Education*. Pennsylvania: Pennsylvania Department of Education.

Herman, Joan L., Pamela R. Aschbacher, Lynn Winters. 1992. *A Practical Guide to Alternative Assessment*. Alexandria: ASCD.

Jacobs, Heidi Hayes. 1989. "The Growing Need for Interdisciplinary Curriculum Content." Chapter 1 of *Interdisciplinary Curriculum: Design and Implementation*. Alexandria: ASCD.

Perkins, David N. 1989. "Selecting Fertile Themes for Integrated Learning." Chapter 6 of *Interdisciplinary Curriculum: Design and Implementation*. Alexandria: ASCD.

Reimer, Bennett. 1989. *A Comprehensive Arts Curriculum, Model, Design for Arts Education*, (July/August).

Bibliography: Arts Across the Curriculum

Anderson, William and Patricia Shehan Campbell. 1989. *Multicultural Perspectives in Music Education*. Reston, VA: Music Educators National Conference.

Anderson, William and Joy Lawrence. 1985. *Integrating Music into the Classroom*. Belmont, CA: Wadsworth Publishing Co.

Campbell, Bruce, Linda Campbell, and Dee Dickinson. 1992. *Teaching and Learning through Multiple Intelligences*. Stanwood, WA: New Horizons for Learning.

Dunleavy, Deborah. 1992. *The Language Beat*. Portsmouth, NH: Heinemann Press.

Gilbert, Ann Green. 1977. *Teaching the Three Rs through Movement Experiences*. Minneapolis, MN: Burgess.

Katz, Susan A., and Judith A. Thomas. 1992. *Teaching Creatively by Working the Word: Language, Music, and Movement*. Englewood Cliffs: Prentice Hall.

Harp, Barbara. 1988. "When the Principal Asks, 'Why Are Your Kids Singing during Reading Time?'" *The Reading Teacher*, January, 454–55.

Lamme, Linda L. 1990. "Exploring the World of Music through Picture Books." *The Reading Teacher*, 44(4), 294–300.

Lazear, D. 1991. *Seven Ways of Knowing*. Tucson, AZ: Zephyr Press.

_____. 1992. *Seven Ways of Teaching*. Tucson, AZ: Zephyr Press.

Upitis, Rena. 1992. *Can I Play You My Song?* (The compositions and invented notations of children.) Portsmouth, ME: Heinemann.

Walker, Pam Prince. 1993. *Bring in the Arts: Lessons in Dramatics, Arts, and Story Writing for Elementary and Middle School Classrooms*. Portsmouth, ME: Heinemann.

Wagner, Betty Jane. 1976. *Dorothy Heathcote: Drama as a Learning Medium*. Washington, DC: NEA Publication.

Werner, Peter H. and Elsie C. Burton. 1979. *Learning through Movement*. St. Louis: C.V. Mosby Co.

Plato Karafelis and Robert I. Hugh discuss integrated arts and integrated curriculum in action at Wolcott Elementary School (Connecticut) where they serve as principal and general music specialist respectively. Their commitment to integrated, student-centered learning stems from a theory that "children should see themselves as creative producers and problem solvers" who are "qualified to comment on the human condition." Citing as a precedent Dewey's idea of school as a model of society, Karafelis and Hugh illustrate the learning culture and environment of an elementary school in which the arts are both integral and integrated.

Integrated Arts and Music Composition at Wolcott Elementary School

By Plato Karafelis and Robert I. Hugh

In the early part of this century, millions of European immigrants arrived at Ellis Island each year. To fully Americanize these people, our education institutions built schools based on the most advanced technology of the time—the factory model. The idea was to box them up, move them through, and after twelve years produce a totally American product.

Unfortunately, after nearly a hundred years, the ideology of those times remains with us. Schools are still built to resemble efficient, production-line factories: Teachers stand at the front of the room and do most of the talking; and students are placed into inflexible classroom groups of twenty-five or more. The demands of late–twentieth century society are straining under the weight of archaic "factory model" practices.

In retrospect, John Dewey may have been right. In 1900, he proposed that to prepare children for society, schools should be structured to resemble society, not factories. Unfortunately,

the legislators and big-business barons of the day prevailed, and we have been mired in their restricted ideology for the past ninety-four years. More frightening still is the prospect that the "outcome-based education" initiatives of legislators and big-business concerns will once again plunge us down the road to educational and social misalignment. Children are not products. Schools are not factories.

Because we feel Dewey was right, Wolcott Elementary School has been designed to resemble society. We have a fully functional student government and an economy based on a federal reserve treasury system. Teachers are empowered through a faculty senate that makes most of the important decisions that affect the school. Parents also sit on the faculty senate. Among other things, we have a theater repertory company, dance repertory company, music studio, post office, researchers, judges, mathematicians, poets, playwrights, town meetings, band, orchestra, choir, patrol guards, school store, audio tech engineers, and recycling system. All our employees are under the age of eleven.

We employ a highly integrated approach to the curriculum. Integrated and cocurricular activities exist across all subject areas; however, the arts seem to offer the best alternative for

Plato Karafelis is principal at Wolcott Elementary School in West Hartford, Connecticut, and Robert I. Hugh is the vocal music teacher at Wolcott Elementary School.

providing meaningful motivation. The arts are part of the natural order when it comes to children and learning.

Philosophically, most schools are places where the relatively young go to watch the relatively old perform. At Wolcott, we believe that school is a place where the relatively young express themselves and the relatively old bend the curriculum to meet that expression. That philosophical shift is critical to our mission; it helps foster the attitude that children are valuable and must be validated each day if they are to become healthy, functional contributors to society. The current push toward outcome-based education will produce readers. Will they be literate? Will they be compassionate? Will they possess the empathy required to overcome the prejudice that has plagued our nation throughout its history? Where is the test that can force compassion, literacy, and empathy into the curriculum? John Dewey was right.

How Did We Start?

How did you start? This is the question we are asked most often. The answer is very simple—you must start with a building principal. The building principal controls what happens in the school, just as the teacher controls what happens in the classroom, and just as the parent controls what happens in the home. If the principal has a vision, your school will move forward. If you do not like that vision, work with the principal to move that vision forward.

Six years ago I was appointed principal at Wolcott School. My vision stems from Dewey's ideas about the school as society. They are seminal and they make good common sense. Our first faculty meeting was scheduled for a hot day at the end of August. This is the meeting where the principal conducts all of the important business and answers all of the important questions for the year that lies ahead. How many copies will we be allowed on the copy machine? Will we be given keys to the building? What is the policy on the use of the laminating machine?

I had never been a principal before, but my natural instinct told me that these were not the critical issues. So instead of discussing the copy policy, we pushed all of the tables back and performed a short play by Isaac Bashevis Singer called *Herschel Gets a Meal*. The play is only one page long.

First, we discussed Isaac Bashevis Singer. Most staff members did not know that he had won the Pulitzer Prize. Most staff members did not know that he wrote short stories about little Russian villages. Many staff members had never heard of him. We performed the play without sets, costumes, or props. We did use sound-effects instruments similar to those used for the old radio plays. The play was so short we performed it several times. We kept changing protagonists and antagonists. One time, we made the narrator the antagonist. We all enjoyed a long laugh.

When we had completed the activity, I asked the staff members a few questions. Did you learn something new today? Did you learn about Isaac Bashevis Singer? Did you learn about protagonist and antagonist relationships? Did you learn that it is easy to do short plays with no sets, costumes, or props? Did you have fun?

As you can imagine, this was the most exciting first-day meeting they had ever had. I then proceeded to ask the central and most critical questions.

"Do you think kids would enjoy doing this?"

They responded with an enthusiastic, "Yes!"

"Do you think kids would learn from this type of approach?"

"Yes!"

"Good, because this is the way we are going to teach at Wolcott from this day forward. If you like this approach, great. If you like it but you're scared, don't worry because the rest of us will help you along. If you are diametrically opposed to this idea, you need to find a way to leave this building as soon as possible." I attempted to be a clear communicator. Six years later, the school is well along the road to becoming everything that John Dewey dreamed more than ninety years ago.

Beliefs

There are certain beliefs that are critical to the success of our school. Beliefs cannot be mandated; they must be acculturated over time. People need time to bring their attitudes into alignment with new belief systems, because our attitudes are firmly rooted in our beliefs about what is best for children.

Teaching is not a job. It is a calling. If you think what we do is a job, please allow me to counsel you out of the profession immediately. You are not serving the needs of your children, their parents, or your colleagues. More important, you are not acknowledging the higher professional and ethical standards that make this the most noble of all professions.

There are people who open doors and there are people who close doors. The word "teacher" is synonymous with the phrase "opening doors to understanding." Yet we all fall into the trap of letting the day-to-day drudgery control our ability to create an impact. Have you ever heard the following door-closing statements? "I would like to, but the schedule won't allow it"; "I would like to, but my principal ..."; or "I would like to, but my team mates ...." Those are classics. Try to catch yourself and others when they exhibit this attitude. Use the following statement as a verbal tool when negotiating with colleagues, "John, you are closing a door!" People who regard our profession as just another job are door closers. Teachers are door openers.

Every child can learn. Sitting Bull once said, "I do not understand the white man. He hits his children and pets his dogs." Some people assign very low esteem to children. It is astounding to find colleagues who believe that some children are not capable of learning just because they are from an inner-city or foreign culture. It is not the child who is incapable of learning, but the adult who is incapable of teaching.

The child is the curriculum. There was a time when I knew what "the basics" were. They had to do with "reading, writing, and arithmetic." Those "basics" are no longer adequate to meet the needs of our changing society. For many of the children we teach, survival of abuse is a basic. For others, avoiding drugs or AIDS is a basic skill. Problem solving in a world filled with problems is a basic skill of the nineties. The only thing that has remained constant is the child. Hence it makes sense to shift our beliefs and attitudes about the basics and recognize that *the child* is the basic curriculum.

How Does Wolcott School Work?

For the purposes of this paper, we will discuss the writing curriculum as the hub of our school program. The writing curriculum is an appropriate hub. It is facilitated by the teacher. It provides a forum for children to express themselves. It is part of a reading/writing continuum. It provides an opportunity for authentic assessment and gives parents direct insight into their children's ability and effort.

Too often, writing takes what we call the "direct route to the refrigerator." The teacher gives an assignment. The student writes. The teacher corrects. The student rewrites. The teacher gives it a star and the paper goes home to be put on the refrigerator. We believe the refrigerator is a great publishing location for a child's writing; however, when you think of all the possible outlets for writing, the refrigerator is only one of many stops along the way.

Our school has a student editorial board. Their job is to monitor student writing, create outlets, and promote a writing attitude in the school. It is composed of nine students in grades three through five. Students are chosen for the editorial board by submitting essays in the fall. Well–thought out and eloquently written essays are numerous, and the selection process is a difficult one. We usually have someone such as a local professional writer evaluate the essays. Students who are selected for the editorial board are then trained to be skilled editors by local writers. Our curriculum specialist is the group's adviser.

The editorial board meets once a week during the school day. Their task is to evaluate the hundreds of pieces of writing that are submitted each week to the magical mailbox. Any student, teacher, parent, or community member may submit a piece of writing to the magical mailbox. The magical mailbox is a funny looking box that sits in the lobby. After all the writing has been evaluated, the editorial board sends the best pieces of writing to one of the many outlets we have created for writing in our school.

Students know that sloppiness will earn a rejection from the editorial board. As a result, almost every piece of writing that is submitted has been revised, edited, spell checked and, in some cases, word processed by the student. This is astounding when one considers that during some weeks, we receive hundreds of pieces of writing. Lately, we have been very busy creating new outlets for writing. A few of our outlets for student writing follow:

Dramatic Repertory Company. At Wolcott School, a piece of student writing may be used as a script for our dramatic repertory company or in the regular classroom. Children's writing is usually short and filled with wonderful characters and exotic locations. Little or no memorization is involved. Students of all ability can be successful in this type of activity. If props, sets, and costumes are eliminated, the teacher task becomes much less imposing. The author resides within your building, and he or she is validated and valued by the experience. Here is the student script we are working on right now, written by Carson Oliver, a fourth-grade student in our school:

Hazbad's Handiwork
By Carson Oliver

The world used to be only
Black and white.
However, there was one place where colors
existed.
Within the books written by the mighty sorcerer
Hazbad!
Hazbad decided that life was too dull without
color,
So he opened all his books
And let the colors fly high as the sun goes,
Low as the vast valleys,
Wide as the biggest cornfield,
Small as a hummingbird.

Publication. Student writing is often submitted for publication by the editorial board. Last year, over twenty pieces of writing were published in real journals. We also publish in our weekly newsletter, and this year we are creating our own publishing company. We plan to publish multiple copies of student-written literature collections, including weather poems, math writing, legends, and so on. These would be infused into our literature program. Our experience has shown that sometimes children write the best literature for children.

We also send student writing to Writer's Spotlight, Town Meeting, the Moving Arts Dance Company, and Word Jazz (see the Opportunities for Wolcott Students subhead and the How Wolcott Works sidebar). By the way, many of the activities described above take place during the regular school day. When the editorial board meets to review writing, we consider that a reading/writing period, even though the activity does not occur in the regular classroom. We believe that working as an editor qualifies as a strong academic, critical thinking, and basic skills function. The notion that learning can only take place in the classroom is a classic factory-model perspective. Remember, the child is the curriculum. The "classroom" exists wherever the child happens to be at the moment he or she is engaged in learning.

The Music Composition Process

Students are particularly delighted and enthusiastic about the music composition process. Each year, our school creates a professionally produced cassette comprising about a dozen original songs written by our students. The process revolves around our writing program. We call the project "Wolcott Songs."

"Wolcott Songs" is an on-going, self-selected project where children write their own lyrics and melody. The process is elegant in its simplicity. For example, "Margot" submits a piece of lyrical writing to the magical mailbox. The editorial board refers the writing to our vocal music teacher, Rob Hugh. Margot might also choose an alternate route to gain entrance into the process by simply waiting around for a minute after music class. She tells Mr. Hugh that she has written lyrics or a melodic idea for a song. The following piece is an example of lyrical writing—the first Wolcott Song we produced:

The Wind
By Margot Simpson

I can hear the wind.
Listen to it clanging, banging,
Rattling at the window demanding
To be let in.
I can hear the wind.
One tree's branch is shaking, breaking,
And then falling
Onto the soft earth.
I can hear the wind.
The wind is rolling, strolling,
And then gently blowing
Away.
Now
I can't hear the wind.
Now
The wind is
Gone.

Mr. Hugh and Margot meet one day after school. They talk about the mood of the piece—how the music and words fit together. They look at the first line of the poem, and Margot sings a melody that sounds like the words make her feel. Mr. Hugh asks Margot to put her ideas on tape. If she doesn't own a cassette recorder, she may use the school's at recess or borrow one from a friend. At this point there are no rules—she sings whatever she feels will match the rhythm and emotion of the words.

When the tape is completed Margot brings it to Mr. Hugh and they listen to her ideas. Often the music contains one or two charming, child-like phrases. Occasionally, the song is complete, written from intuition in correct song style. Some children may even attempt to write the music on paper. Margot and Mr. Hugh will discuss her music and he may suggest a few revisions. On more than one occasion, his advice

and strong lobbying have been soundly rejected. Sometimes, children know what they want.

When Margot is satisfied, she and Mr. Hugh find some time to record the song using the school's recording equipment, which consists of a Macintosh computer, a four-track tape recorder, microphones, a MIDI keyboard, and a sound module. Mr. Hugh plays the accompaniment and Margot sings the melody. Sometimes the composer elects to have a friend sing the melody. Picture the scenario: A little first-grade student is wearing a headset that is five times too large for her head. She is standing in front of a microphone and her favorite music teacher, focusing all her energy to the task. They record retake after retake and she never loses her concentration. She knows she is creating a unique product. Her song is special because no one in the world has ever performed this song before. She envisions her song being choreographed and presented by the Moving Arts Dance Company at the town meeting.

When the song is finished, we usually invite the parents in for a private playing. In each and every case, tears fill the eyes. Those tears represent something special. Parents cry because the song is beautiful. It is an accomplishment. It is the result of discipline. It is evidence of their child's literacy and compassion. Most important, however, those tears represent a child who has achieved the potential that Mom and Dad knew he or she possessed all along. We believe that every child can meet his or her potential. We also believe that children are capable of teaching us all to achieve with excellence.

The music composition process is exciting and rewarding. It provides another vehicle for displaying and motivating writing. The collaborative approach of creating the melody is rewarding for the teacher and the student. The student feels pride and increased self-esteem as her words come alive.

At the end of the year the song will be included on a cassette that is copied and given to every family at Wolcott. Some of the songs are played into the computer and a "professional" copy of the song is printed for other musicians to read.

From thought, to paper, to song, to dance, the students' writing evolves and sustains longevity and beauty.

Many of our colleagues have expressed an interest in duplicating this process. They have listened to the tape and have been charmed by the creative ability of children. The artistic potential that is inherent in children, and the willingness to listen and be inspired are what make this process work.

Opportunities for Wolcott Students

Primary (Grades 1–2) and intermediate (Grades 3–5) math clubs—Students gather data (surveys, observations, etc.), crunch data, and present data through graphs, documents, and other means. Math clubs meet on Tuesday or Wednesday morning. This year we plan to offer three-week sessions. (Students write an essay to enter.)

Wolcott Rangers—(Grade 5) This is an environmental science club. They meet each Thursday morning. Much of their work is conducted at Wolcott Park. They make presentations at the town meeting, create displays, and they are agents of environmental repair. (Participants are self-selected.)

Reading Incentive Program—Each year, we select an academic theme for our Reading Incentive Program (RIP). In the past, we have studied mythology, American history, and statehood. A huge display is created in the lobby. As teams read books, they tally the number of pages they have read. The more pages they read, the further along they move in our display. For example, last year we created a statehood time line. Students began in the year 1776, and as they read pages they moved through time to 1959, when Hawaii and Alaska achieved statehood.

The purpose of RIP is to get all students reading. Teams are made up of one primary and one intermediate classroom. The two classrooms get together and read to each other. The emphasis is on quality reading. There are no external incentives. In fact, the first team to fin-

ish goes back and helps the team in last place to move forward more quickly. (All students must join.)

Wee Deliver—(Grades K–5) Our school has an internal post office called Wee Deliver. It is run in conjunction with the U.S. Postal Service. Students and teachers are encouraged to send letters to one another. They must use proper addresses and letters must adhere to a standard letter format. Many classrooms have letter-writing centers. The post office is run by first- and second-grade students. Each month we hire a postmaster, sorters and carriers. (Workers are hired by the teacher coordinator.)

American Sign Language Club—(Grades K–5) This is the first year for the signing club. They will learn sign language and present poems, songs, and stories to the rest of the school at the town meeting. (Students submit an essay.)

The Student Editorial Board—(Grades 3–5) Each year, nine students are selected to sit on the student editorial board. The editorial board is trained by professional writers. They meet once a week to review student writing that has been submitted to them through the magical mailbox. The magical mailbox is a large polka dotted mailbox in the lobby. Anyone from the school community is invited to submit writing to the mailbox.

Students at Wolcott are encouraged to submit writing to the magical mailbox on a regular basis. Good writing is sent on to the Wolcott Repertory Company (REPCO), Moving Arts, the music composition process, or other outlets for publication or presentation. (Students submit a writing portfolio to be selected for the editorial board.)

Student Council—(Grades 3–5 in the fall, Grades 1 & 2 added in the winter) In order to learn responsibility, children must be given the opportunity to handle responsibility. That is one reason Wolcott School has a fully functioning student government program. Students in grades 3 through 5 are elected by their peers. Student council meets on Wednesday afternoons during recess. They create laws. They hire patrol guards. They select supreme court justices. The president is elected by a vote of the entire student body. They are not a puppet government. They are a bona fide decision-making group with wide-ranging responsibility and authority. (Students are elected.)

Supreme Court Judges—(Grades 3–5) Judges are trained in mediation techniques by the principal. Each day, two judges preside over cases that occur during the grades 3 through 5 recess. Judgments are rendered and disciplinary action is taken. A typical punishment is a five-minute recess penalty. Students who swear or fight are sent to the office immediately. Judges are appointed for the entire year. (Students are appointed by the president and confirmed by the senate.)

The Endowed Writer's Chair—(Grade 5) Each year, one or two students are selected, based on merit, to become practicing writers for a period of up to two weeks. All arrangements are made through the cooperation of the parents, teachers, and administration. Endowed writers spend the entire two weeks writing as per a signed contract. The school work that would have been assigned during that time is accomplished via a process called curriculum compacting. At the end of the two weeks, a book of writing is produced and shared via REPCO, the town meeting, and publication. (Students join by invitation only.)

Publication—(Grades K–5) Last year, the writing of approximately twenty Wolcott students was published in journals. We hope to do better each year. (Students are selected by the editorial board.)

Annual Awards Assembly—(Grades 1–5) Each year we hold one awards assembly. In the past, we have presented academic awards. This year, our school community plans to reevaluate the awards program. (Students are selected by the teacher.)

Wolcott Repertory Company (REPCO)—(Grades 1–5) A theater group comprising one student from each classroom. Each child participates for a half year. Students may participate in REPCO twice during their Wolcott career, once in primary (grades 1 & 2) and once in intermediate (grades 3–5). REPCO uses short scripts, and it does not use costumes, sets, or props. Instead, it concentrates on communicating the written word. The students meet before school on Mondays. (Students are selected by the teacher.)

Moving Arts Dance Company—(Grades 4 & 5) Each year, seventeen students from grades four and five are selected for this program. They participate for the entire year. Students create original dance programs using songs composed and performed by other Wolcott students (see Music Composition Process). They also interpret a couple of funky numbers each year. The group meets during recess and during a small part of class time. (Students are selected by audition.)

Music Composition Process—(Grades K–5) Students are encouraged to submit lyrics that result from their writing class or personal writing. If selected by the vocal music teacher, the student then works through the process of melody construction, performance, and studio production. All songs are included on the annual "Wolcott Songs" tape. Each year, Moving Arts interprets several of the songs through dance. Students meet during arranged times. (Students are selected by the vocal music teacher.)

Town Meeting—Each Friday, the entire school comes together in the auditorium for the town meeting. This is a time to share the many arts, academics, and America projects that are ongoing at the school. Regular features of the town meeting include: Writer's Spotlight, Quiz-O-Matic—The Math Game for Kids, Moving Arts, and Works of the Great Masters. (Everyone participates.)

The Poet Warriors—(Grades 3–5) Five students present an original poem as an introduction to Writer's Spotlight at the town meeting each week. The poem may be presented through various techniques including puppetry, theater, dance, mime, or reader's theater. Students will be selected based upon merit, teacher judgment, and talent. (Students are selected by the principal.)

The Bushnell Partners Program—(Grade 1) Wolcott School is fortunate to have been chosen as a partner school by the Bushnell. Through this program, our school will work with a series of teaching and performing artists to explore issues of literacy and diversity. The grant has been endowed for a ten-year period. (Open to all grade-1 students.)

Wordjazz—Three or four times a year we sponsor a wordjazz concert. Students are encouraged to submit writing to the magical mailbox. The student editorial board selects a dozen written pieces from the hundreds that are submitted. A jazz trio or quartet is invited to the school. The whole school goes to the auditorium, and children whose written works were selected are called to the front to share their writing. They select instruments, moods, and tempos, and we instantly interpret their writing as song. (Everyone participates and student writing is selected by the student editorial board.)

The Annual Student/Faculty Original Musical—(Grade 4 & 5 choir students) Each year, students and faculty produce and perform an original musical play. Students and teachers work together on the production. Rehearsals are held before school. (Participants audition.)

Works of the Great Masters—(Grades 1–5) This group of five students selects, researches, and interprets three pieces of visual art for presentation at the town meeting approximately once a month. (Students are selected by the principal and the art teacher.)

Reader's Theater—A weekly component of the town meeting. A small group of students interpret a short piece of writing in the style of the old radio plays. Sound effects included.

Performing Arts Festival—(Grades 3–5) Each year eight students in grades 3–5 are selected to write and present an original play/story at the Connecticut Storyteller's Performing Arts Festival. The festival is held in May. They rehearse outside of the school day. (Students write an essay or are selected by the teacher coordinator.)

Band and Orchestra—(Grades 4 & 5) All fourth- and fifth-grade students are encouraged to take instrumental music lessons at school. Lessons are offered to each student for thirty minutes per week. Students studying string instruments receive two thirty-minute lessons per week. Instrumental students play in the band and orchestra. Band and orchestra meet before school and present two concerts per year. Extra rehearsals are scheduled during class time prior to each concert. (Students are self-selected.)

Choir—(Grades 4 & 5) All fourth- and fifth-grade students are encouraged to participate in choir. Choir meets before school. As with band and orchestra, two concerts are presented each year and extra rehearsals are scheduled during class time prior to each concert. (Students are self-selected.)

The Design Team—(Grades 1–5) Each year, five to ten students are selected for the design team. Students who wish to be considered must submit a portfolio of art work that meets established criteria. The design team facilitates the school's graphics program. They design concert programs, logos, and select artwork for special programs and projects. (Students submit a portfolio to the art teacher.)

Patrol Guards—(Grades 1–5) Student patrol guards help us maintain an environment that is quiet, safe, and conducive to learning. They patrol the hallways before school and during recess, and they also help run bus dismissal. Patrol guards wear florescent orange patrol belts. (Guards hired by the student council.)

Four-Square Tournament—(Grades 3–5) Each fall, we sponsor a four-square tournament. The tournament is held during recess. The tournament is designed to teach the game to students so that they will be involved in organized play at recess. It is an individual sport and offers a nice alternative to children who are looking for a way to fit in or make friends. (Students are self-selected.)

School Store—(Grades K–5) The school store is open every Monday and Thursday morning before school beginning at 8:25. Students may use real money or Wolcoins to purchase pencils, notebooks, erasers, and other small items. The

How Wolcott Works

- There are thirty-six different opportunities available to students at Wolcott.
- There are a wide variety of options for gaining entrance into one of the student opportunities. They are designed to reflect the skills that children will need to be successful in the real world. These options are for the student to:
  - Submit an essay
  - Be selected by the teacher
  - Be elected
  - Audition
  - Select themselves
  - Join a group in which everyone participates
  - Be selected randomly
  - Be selected by the editorial board
  - Be appointed
  - Be appointed and confirmed by the senate
  - Submit a proposal
  - Submit a portfolio
  - Be invited
  - Be selected based on merit.
- Thirteen opportunities take place before school
- Thirteen opportunities take place during school
- Six opportunities take place during recess
- One opportunity takes place after school
- Three opportunities take place before, during, and after school
- The thirty-six opportunities provide more than 3,000 slots that children will occupy during the course of the year.

store is located in the library. It is run by students. School store profits are used to buy books for the library. (Cashiers and manager are selected by the media specialist.)

Student of the Month—(Grades K–5) Each month, each class selects a student of the month. Classmates discuss why that child is worthy of the distinction. In the fall, we survey the class to find out how many times each student has received this recognition. That information is factored into the choice. (Students are randomly selected or chosen by the teacher.)

The Welcome Choir—(Grades 4 & 5) Visitors to the building are greeted by a small choir. They sing a short song of welcome and then offer a personal welcome to the school. (Students are selected by the vocal teacher.)

The Techmeisters, Audio-Tech Crew—(Grade 5) Two students run the sixteen-channel sound board and lighting system for town meeting, assemblies, and concerts. (Students are selected by the vocal teacher, the classroom teacher, and the principal.)

Gymnastics Club—(Grades 2–5) Our physical education teachers offer gymnastics to all interested students. The gymnastics club meets three mornings and three afternoons per week. Students may also practice during recess. Several times a year, they present their skills to parents at an evening event. Periodically, the gymnastics club joins Duffy School and both schools present a joint display of skills. Last year, a documentary was produced during our gymnastics show and was presented on local-access television. (Students are self-selected.)

Recycle Team—(Grades 1–5) Wolcott School recycles all white paper. Each Tuesday morning the recycle team collects recycle bins and brings the paper to a central location. The paper is then picked up by the recycle company. Twenty students from all grades are selected to serve on the recycle team. (Students are selected by the classroom teacher.)

Running Club—(Grades 4–5) Similar to the gymnastics club, students meet beyond the school day to run for better health. The program is run by our physical education staff. (Students are self-selected.)

PTA Talent Show—(Grades K–5) Each year, we host a huge talent show. All students are able to participate. We have strict rules for participation to ensure quality. Students must audition and mentors are assigned to all acts. A dress rehearsal is held. Everyone has a great time, and there are many tears of laughter and joy. It is designed to be fun. (Students are self-selected.)

Junior Jazzercise—(Grades 3–5) There is a possibility of developing this club for this year. They would meet one time per week before or after school.

Conclusion

When it comes to educating children, we should ask ourselves, "To what end?"

Is it enough that they learn to read, write, and compute? Perhaps not. We believe children should also see themselves as creative producers and problem solvers; we believe that children should understand that they are qualified to comment on the human condition; that they are not alone; that they can communicate with others; that they are valued and valuable; that they are compassionate, literate, and empathic beings who have something to offer; that happiness is derived from a good education, a strong family, hard work, and caring for your fellow human beings. Sometimes *knowing* you can make a difference is all the motivation a person needs to go out and *make* a difference. These are the really important lessons. These are the lessons that teach someone to do something with his or her life—to leave the world a better place than the world one came into.

Section 3

Reflections and Applications

Opportunities for thoughtful exchange of ideas among music educators are often limited by the circumstances of our working environments. Frequently, music teachers are one of only a few arts educators and sometimes the sole music professional in a school. Richness of ideas developed in communities of general music educators and arts educators are important to the growth of both the individual and the profession. During the symposium, groups of music teachers met in Reflections and Applications discussion groups to exchange ideas and react to the presentations by the symposium speakers.

The five articles in this section, by discussion group leaders, summarize the reactions, thinking, recommendations, and concerns of the general music educators who attended the symposium. Wendy L. Sims outlines the discussions of music educators interested in the early childhood years. Phyllis Kaplan and Judith Theiss summarize the thoughts of elementary general music educators. Concerns of middle school general music teachers are reflected in the article by Jacquelyn Boswell. June Hinckley focuses on issues that affect general music educators and programs in the high school. Discussions from a group of music educators considering a wide range of constituencies from college through adulthood are summarized by David Myers and Chelcy Bowles. The recommendations generated by the Reflections and Applications discussion groups are a call to action for each reader, for every general music educator in the nation. If we wish to be part of the schools of the future, we must also be part of the educational reform movement today.

Wendy L. Sims summarizes the thoughts of music educators who attended the symposium's early childhood discussion group. Sims addresses the challenges and issues of music education for young children, including early intervention, diversity of settings, informing others both within and outside of the music education profession, delivery of instruction, and the role of technology. Recommendations from the early childhood group challenge music educators to seek and develop new opportunities for enriching the lives of our youngest learners with music.

Early Childhood Discussion-Group Report

By Wendy L. Sims

A core group of about eighteen people attended the early childhood discussion sessions, including primarily elementary school music teachers and college/university music education faculty plus several school or program administrators. This report summarizes the issues discussed and conclusions drawn by this candid, lively, constructive group.

We were gratified to hear of the emphasis placed on music in early childhood by several of the guest speakers at this symposium. Sometimes it seems as if colleagues outside our profession have been quicker to acknowledge the importance of music in early childhood than many of our colleagues within the field.

While the importance of reaching young children musically was not in question in our group, the challenges of doing so were a major topic of concern. We addressed the role of music in early childhood education, uses of computer technology, and recommendations for MENC and the profession.

Wendy L. Sims is associate professor of music education at the University of Missouri–Columbia.

Challenges of Influencing the Music Education of Young Children

Our primary delivery system is not through the traditional music specialist, but through the adults that care for young children on a regular basis. Much of the responsibility for children's early music experiences resides with the staff at all types of childcare facilities—from home care to early-intervention programs to day-care centers to preschools operated by public schools. Parents (and perhaps grandparents) also must play a major role, because perhaps at no other period do they have such an important influence on their children's development. Because there is no centralized structure for reaching children before they become part of the formal education system, our challenge lies in developing innovative ways to influence and assist all of the adults who interact regularly with young children.

Unfortunately, another group that we still need to reach is our music education and professional musician colleagues. It appears to us that many of these have not yet realized that the experiential basis of music education starts at birth (and maybe even before). Even though they may not be directly involved in working with young children, there are many ways these people can be more overtly helpful and supportive, including assisting those in their community who do provide music experiences for young children. For example, they can be advocates for quality music programs in their own children's preschool settings, demonstrate their instruments for young children (or take their students to do this), present age-appropriate children's concerts, or make presentations to groups that they have contact with, such as parent-teacher organizations, who might reach younger children not yet in school.

Music educators must stop thinking about and referring to ourselves in terms of "K–12." If we really believe in lifelong learning, then music education should be a "birth-through-life" proposition.

The Role of Music in Early Childhood

Music belongs throughout the child's day in many capacities. The arts are integrated into the young child's life. Children need music play and unsquelched spontaneous music making. We also believe, however, that they need group music time to experience the important social and musical aspects of sharing music and making music together.

To deliver this will require either early childhood arts specialists as full-time staff members at centers and preschools, or, because that may be a bit idealistic, the following two-part alternative: First, better training and in-service for childcare workers. Early childhood professionals are our allies. They want music for their children—they value music, but are very insecure about their own musical abilities. That is why the second component of this plan is important: visiting music specialists with training in child development to provide musicality and creativity and to serve as models and consultants for the childcare staff.

The Role of Computer Technology in Early Childhood Music Education

Computer technology was an important theme of the symposium, and many interesting and exciting new developments were presented. What is the appropriate role of computers for early childhood music education? We concluded

that this technology should not serve as a substitute for actual, concrete, hands-on experiences with music, musical instruments, and musicians. It could be, however, a valuable supplement to the early childhood music curriculum if the programs are interactive and exploratory in nature.

Recommendations for MENC and the Profession

As a result of our discussions, we developed a number of recommendations for future development. Since we believe it is becoming clearer and clearer that our profession has much to gain from ensuring that children receive quality musical experiences from the earliest years, we believe that MENC should take a leadership role in promoting and developing these ideas and initiatives.

These recommendations are based on the following premise: Music educators must "infiltrate" the community of those adults who directly control young children's environments; we must find a way to have an impact on young children's musical experiences and development. To achieve this goal:

■ We must work more closely—even aggressively—with the national professional early childhood organizations (National Association for the Education of Young Children; Association for Early Childhood International). Possible approaches are through articles and advertisements in their publications, program sessions and displays at their conferences, and even direct mailings to their membership.

■ Music educators need to become a force in the popular press. For example, articles might be published in magazines such as *Good Housekeeping* or *Parents Magazine,* or even articles such as "Quality Musical Gifts for Grandchildren" in an AARP (American Association of Retired Persons) publication or similar magazine.

■ We need to seek opportunities for involvement in community outreach programs such as parenting classes, prenatal classes, and parents-as-teachers organizations. Even pediatricians' waiting rooms provide a possible forum for educational materials. More ambitious ideas include finding a corporate sponsor to send a cassette tape produced by music educators home with every new parent.

■ We need to bring music from the community into the preschool settings. A network of community musicians, whether professionals, amateurs, parents, grandparents, or even high school students could be developed by, and receive instruction from, local music educators (perhaps with materials developed by MENC). This volunteer "music corps" could then be available to interact with children in the various childcare settings.

■ Music educators should be able to recommend or provide materials such as a discography of quality children's music, videotapes of appropriate adult/child music interactions, brochures and printed materials for parents and childcare programs, and so on. MENC should take a leadership role in the production and distribution of these materials.

■ We need to develop, provide, and promote age-appropriate musical materials that represent cultural and ethnic diversity.

■ The profession needs much more research on the role and impact of music in the early years, so that we may speak with more authority and be certain that our programs are based on developmentally appropriate models and principles.

■ We must find ways to have some impact and influence on the mass media. We need to learn from the extraordinary appeal of media phenomena such as the television hit program "Barney" (no matter how adults may feel about it). We must analyze the qualities that appeal so strongly to children (e.g., simplicity, repetition, warmth, and security) and identify what we perceive to be problems (e.g., lack of variety of musical material, quality of children's vocal production). Then we need to make an effort to improve, from a music education perspective, the musical content in the media aimed at young children, perhaps with a letter-writing campaign, with personal contacts when possible, or with our influence as a major professional organization.

Conclusions

Young children learn in an integrated world of exploring, playing, experiencing, and interacting with their environment. The term "general music" with its traditional connotations actually is not relevant to early childhood. Perhaps "music experiences" would be a preferable designation, or, thinking of an analogy to the whole language movement, maybe even "whole music."

Children are naturally musical. They initiate musical activities and behave in musical ways from waking up until bedtime. We need to find avenues and form partnerships to nurture and sustain the joy of music making and to develop and encourage children's innate musicality and interest. This is a critical issue for our profession, because the foundation for lifelong music learning is built in early childhood.

The elementary general music discussion group, led by Phyllis Kaplan and Judith Theiss, addressed a broad range of issues, ideas, and concerns important to music educators working with children in the elementary grades. Kaplan and Theiss summarize reactions to symposium speakers and discussions about assessment, cultural diversity, and the integration of music with other subjects. Recommendations from the elementary general music group call for initiatives that support positive change and improvement in elementary general music instruction.

Music Education and Elementary School

By Phyllis Kaplan and Judith Theiss

The Elementary General Music discussion group wishes to thank MENC and the Society for General Music for making possible this wonderful exchange of ideas. Our discussion group—fifty-four elementary general music educators from thirty-two states—met four times throughout the symposium to respond to presentations and to make recommendations for further action. This report highlights the work of our group.

We identified a number of concerns that are central to the tomorrow we envision for elementary general music. Four main themes emerged throughout the days of the symposium:

■ The relationship between music instruction and the overall growth and development of students.

■ The effect of technology on the teaching of general music in the twenty-first century.

■ The importance of basing music learning experiences on repertoire that reflects the cultural diversity of our times.

■ The connections among music, its social

Phyllis Kaplan is coordinator of general and choral music for the Montgomery County (MD) Public Schools, and Judith Theiss is a general/choral music teacher in the same school system.

purpose, general education, and American culture.

Gene Carter's thoughtful introduction to the symposium provided us with a lens through which to filter all of the issues and decisions we face in restructuring and reforming elementary general music for the twenty-first century when he said, "The degree to which we meet the needs of all students will determine how successful we are." Carter acknowledged that music education has been strongly aligned with the goals of school reform all along because of its focus on performance. He praised music education's ability to help students develop thinking skills and problem-solving abilities that will influence their lifelong success.

Jane Healy's central thesis was that music education processes are critical to the growth and development of children. She cited music as a powerful "brain builder and brain integrator," arguing the importance of music in the curriculum by stating that the twenty-first century will demand synthesis of sequential, analytical, and holistic skills—skills that are well developed in musicians. Healy addressed the importance of retaining childhood in a technical society, noting that research indicates that today's environments are having a negative influence on children's ability to concentrate, analyze, and think critically and creatively. She spoke about her fear that today's "computer kids" are lacking the kinds of hands-on, cooperative activities that promote sensory development, a critical element in brain growth. Her recommendations included providing hands-on experiences with music that include singing, listening, and moving—as early as age two. She noted that it is important to provide a strong auditory base as the foundation for reading (paralleling the "rote before note" philosophy common to general music methodology).

Morton Subotnick demonstrated the close relationship between the process of composing and the process of learning music. Using software and CD-ROM programs, he illustrated a technological form of hands-on experimentation with sound, showing how this technology offers an alternative way to interact directly with musical elements that has not been possible for students with limited music performance skills.

There was some controversy in our group discussions regarding the compatibility of Jane Healy's and Morton Subotnick's views, but many felt that Healy's statement regarding hands-on experiences as the foundation for abstract thought provided a strong rationale for the kinds of interactive computer experiences Subotnick advocated.

Another issue addressed by the discussion group was that "technology addiction" could present a threat to the performance curriculum. Most participants agreed that the impact on performance programs could be positive because of the increased conceptual understanding and motivation resulting from a balanced instructional program that takes advantage of technology. The group consensus was that technology is another instructional tool that can enhance music instruction and provide increased community support and understanding of our general music program.

A strong element of a new vision for general music was described in Charles Fowler's new paradigm of value-centered music education. Fowler cited statistics that provided us with a wake-up call to the fact that music has become "increasingly tangential in American education

since the 1960s." In an attempt to restore music to a place of high value and importance in our society, Fowler proposed the reconnecting of music to general education, to its social purpose, and to American culture.

In speaking to the reconnection of music to general education, Fowler encouraged teachers to focus on music as part of a general education so that it serves as a source of value and understanding for all people, not just a talented elite. He asked us to be wary of emphasizing technique at the expense of meaning as we work to reconnect music to its social purpose. Fowler also urged music educators to reconnect music with American culture by exploring the relationship of music to the ethnicity of our students, treating music as a means of building bridges between people. Our discussion group heartily endorsed those recommendations.

Other discussions centered on assessment, cultural diversity, and the integration of music with other subjects. Participants cited many reasons for expanded cultural diversity in the elementary music education curriculum, primarily the opportunity to acquire broadened musical experience and the development of respect for others. There was general agreement that assessment is an integral part of the teaching process and that we must continue to explore ways of evaluating our program and its effect on students. The integration of music with other subjects was seen as a way to make learning more holistic for students and demonstrating the importance of music in the total curriculum. There were strong expressions that successful interdisciplinary programs always respect the uniqueness and integrity of each subject.

Although we were concerned and frustrated by the realities and limitations of our daily teaching situations, the elementary general music educators agreed that the development of a new vision should not be constrained by those limitations. We were committed to the premise that change is a necessary and exciting process that will result in our professional growth as well as in our ability to enable all students to realize their musical potential.

We believe that we are obliged to find the frameworks, establish the models, and locate the support we need to make the changes that point us toward our vision for tomorrow. In that spirit, we share with you some words you have heard before, in a different context—"If you build it, they will come!"

Recommendations

1. The recommendations of this symposium should be considered as a high priority by MENC, which should support our intentions to become agents of change for improved elementary general music instruction.

2. Follow-up seminars to continue the work of this symposium should be planned.

3. Music educators should give credibility to the music of students' culture, and consider using it as a starting point for the study of all music. Learning environments that include familiar sounds and genres can help students see "school" music as "real" music.

4. Electronic media should play an integral role in general music instruction, providing the basis for non–teacher centered problem solving that nurtures musical independence in the learner.

5. Pre- and in-service programs should equip elementary general music educators to include electronic media in their repertoire of instructional strategies.

6. World music should be part of a balanced, broadly based elementary general music repertoire.

7. Undergraduate programs in music education should include required courses in world music as well as methods courses that prepare future teachers to use this repertoire. School systems and graduate music education programs should continue this commitment to professional growth.

8. The elementary general music curriculum must be child-centered and reflect a sensitivity to appropriate developmental practice.

9. The elementary general music curriculum must be connected to the other subjects in ways that preserve its integrity and promote more holistic learning.

10. Elementary music educators must connect their curriculum more closely to other school programs, the community at large, and other professional leadership organizations.

Jacquelyn Boswell presents a summary of the discussions and recommendations of the middle school discussion group. Key issues for the group were the unique developmental characteristics of the middle school learner and the value of knowing and performing music for students in the middle grades. Recommendations point to greater exploration of community resources, more connections to academic teams and other parts of the school community, and improved initial and continuing education for members of the profession who teach general music in the middle school.

Reflections and Applications for Middle School

By Jacquelyn Boswell

Nearly two hundred general music teachers met at the Society for General Music (SGM) Symposium and took advantage of a rare opportunity to reflect upon issues germane to our field. Thought-provoking addresses from inside and outside our professional circle served as catalysts for multilevel discussion groups. Gene Carter and Jane Healy began as plenary speakers, clearly recognizing the importance of the arts as a more powerful universal than is recognized by most (see pages 11 and 15); Charles Fowler followed with his usual eloquence and beautifully articulated straight talk about the future of music education (see page 21); and Morton Subotnick showed us exciting new possibilities with technology (see page 31). Finally, Sally Monsour's poignant retrospective illustrating why we do the things we do capped off many memorable events (see page 43). This first symposium for general music educators was a major success in unfolding the breadth and diversity of views about curricular goals and activities, important musical concepts, utilitarian and pragmatic purposes, and the varied approaches to general music education.

Recent movements toward educational reform, the schools of tomorrow, and the identification of National Standards served as a pervasive undercurrent in addresses and discussions. All participants were given ample opportunity to share ideas, visions, and concerns. Four breakout sessions were interspersed for the individual interest groups with participants representing all MENC regions.

Our group, Middle School Level, spent productive time in small discussion groups. Each member brought issues and challenges to the discussion. The topics were as broad as they were diverse, ranging from visionary ideas and perceptions in the current reform movement to specific local problem areas.

Two major themes running through our issue-oriented discussions were the uniqueness of the middle school learner, coupled with the value of knowing and performing music. One of the most popular recommendations for music education addressed the need for all music education majors (instrumental, choral, and general music) to have a course in middle level general music.

Before the conclusion of the symposium, we identified some major recommendations for general music practitioners, SGM, MENC, and teacher preparation. Our mission statement is this:

Jacquelyn Boswell is professor of music at Arizona State University–Tempe.

As educators we believe that middle school general music must be recognized as a critical and central component of the middle school core curriculum. Therefore, the mission of the general music class is to provide all learners with opportunities for appreciating, understanding, evaluating, creating, and performing music to ensure lifelong learning and enjoyment of music.

Following are the recommendations made for professional practice in view of research, restructuring, and reform:

■ Offer learning opportunities for making essential connections through social context and world themes.

■ Strive to establish strategies and procedures for students to undergo criticism and analysis.

■ Provide memorable, substantive instruction for long-range educational benefits.

■ Provide age-appropriate depth of instruction for the formal learning stage of early adolescent students.

■ Be an active forum to adapt appropriate applications of new technology.

■ Use educational terminology and the vocabulary common to all middle school educators to describe the early adolescent learner as a whole child.

■ Draw assessment and evaluation practices from content and concepts of balanced, sequenced curricula.

Many ideas emerged during our work sessions and discussions to further the cause of general music:

1. *Seek out resources in the community that can be advantageous to the general music program.* This can be especially fruitful when the general music teacher needs some authentic demonstrations of music and dance from other cultures and finds them among parents, school personnel, and at community or religious centers. Seeking the resources of retirees with expertise in music and leisure time to assist in the instructional arena can be an intergenerational benefit to all involved. Also, local industries could be tapped for assistance providing low-cost com-

puter technology and software. Having citywide and statewide resource centers for general music materials and instruments would also greatly enhance the general music teacher's cache of resources.

2. *Work to become part of academic teams to develop a core-integrated curriculum.* Symposium participants at the middle school level felt that the value of music is too understated and little known, and the music curriculum is too isolated from the middle school curriculum. Everyone agreed that all efforts must be dedicated to make music practices known to the school staff and parents. They also expressed the need to shift the focus of music education from its isolation as a satellite, a peripheral course, to a core curriculum class. As Charles Fowler had urged, many stated the need to form partnerships with other subjects to diminish the perception of an isolated, tangential curriculum in music. Efforts to coordinate the music curriculum with other subjects need not be large projects initially but small thematic-centered ideas. Integrated instruction calls for the general music instructor to seek modes of multidisciplinary integration within the music class, as well as with colleagues, with other art forms, and with other disciplines.

3. *All music educators need preservice and in-service general music courses.* We have witnessed many instances where general music classes are being taught by graduates from certification programs who have had no prior experience or education in general music. In some cases teachers of performing groups have been reassigned without any general music preparation being required. If all music educators are to understand and embrace general music as the core of the curriculum, intended to involve all students regardless of previous musical experience in a comprehensive music curriculum, teacher-preparation institutions must require all music education majors to enroll in general music course work. Topics that especially need addressing for middle level teaching in preparatory courses and workshops are developmental processes of adolescents; age-appropriate concepts and activities; accommodations for special-needs students;

lessons that illustrate collaborative grouping, problem solving, questioning techniques, and risk taking; and resources and technology.

4. *Should the term "general music" be changed?* Some feel that the term lacks focus, specificity, stature, and communication of its meaning. As someone pointed out, however, Mary Hoffman has said on numerous occasions, "There's nothing general about general music!" It was suggested that a name change might be appropriate at the local level to identify specific course names; that is, individual schools may find it advantageous to use inviting course titles that best describe the nature of the content. As examples, some options might be Music & Culture, Music Perspectives, Problem-Solving in Music, Thinking Musically, Technology & Music, Introduction to Guitar, Composing Film Scores, and so forth.

5. *It is strongly recommended that MENC and the Society for General Music are a part of the facilitation of the new directions and reform efforts.* Our discussion group made two specific requests of SGM and MENC: host another symposium in the near future to address additional concerns with a broader representation of general music educators; and publish professional development materials, especially those that provide strategies for us to become agents for change in and out of our immediate profession. In addition, we need publications on developmental phases of adolescence, making transfer of learning to new situations, and problem-solving models, to name a few. We also need state and regional assistance with developing a network to share projects already developed by others.

6. *Greater assurance is needed that music edu-cators are adequately prepared to teach general music.* Recommendations from the middle school level participants at the symposium include the following:

■ At least one course should be required for all music education undergraduate students to study general music methodology and resources.

■ Frequent in-service workshops in general music should be held for the increasing number of instrumental and choral directors who are teaching general music without undergraduate preparation. Workshops in secondary general music also appear to be needed, based on the increasing number of states requiring a fine arts component for high school graduation.

■ It was also recommended that preparation for school administrators include an arts component. In many districts, school principals and administrators make major decisions about curriculum, personnel, and budget without benefit of expertise. Contacting faculty in administration courses and requesting time to address matters on administration of music programs was suggested.

In summary, this symposium represents the first effort by MENC to gather general music educators outside the biennial conferences. Participants felt passionate about new directions in general music and wished to urge our colleagues to make connections and form new partnerships, especially to better advertise what we contribute to education and to the personal expression gained by our students. The participants expressed their gratitude to the presidents of MENC and SGM for their vision and implementation of the symposium along with sincere wishes that both organizations start an immediate plan for a follow-up symposium.

June Hinckley summarizes the reflections of the high school discussion group. Curricula relevant to student's lives and interests and connected with their cultures and communities are critical to success in high school general music courses or general music components of performance classes. The group's recommendations focus on curriculum diversity and teacher preparation as key elements for a new vision of high school general music.

Issues in High School General Music

By June Hinckley

In our group, representatives from the university level, music supervisors, teachers newly involved in teaching general music at the high school level, and teachers with a lot of successful experience focused on issues in high school general music. A number of the experienced teachers had incorporated general music practices into some of their performance classes with a great deal of success. The discussion ranged from very practical "how to" matters to philosophical issues to the impact of reform on the entire high school program. So that the group would immediately focus on some of the current issues in music as well as education in general, the following questions formed the basis for the early discussion that occurred in this session:

1. Often the students who take general music in high school have not taken any music since elementary school. What type of program of study do you think would be most appealing and meaningful to them?

2. For years music appreciation was considered to be general music for the secondary student. The research, however, supports a more hands-on, performance-oriented approach. What should be the orientation of the high school general music program of study—performance or music appreciation?

3. Popular music is a vital part of the life of most high school students. What is the role of popular music in the high school general music program?

4. The National Standards deal with creating and performing, perceiving and analyzing, and understanding cultural and historical contexts. Can all of this be covered, let alone learned, by high school general music students?

5. Some students come to general music classes with a rich background in music and some know very little about music. How does the teacher deal with the varying ability levels of students in high school general music classes?

6. All areas of the curriculum today are having to deal with the practical issues of employability and relevance. How can general music for the high school address these issues?

7. Outcome-Based Education talks about determining what students should know and be able to do. What outcomes can we expect students to know and be able to do with music in their adult lives as a result of having been a high school general music student?

These questions served as the springboard for

June Hinckley is music, fine arts, and instructional strategies specialist at the Florida Department of Education.

our discussion, which eventually led to topics of more particular interest to the group. We quickly discovered that we had all had quite different experiences in teaching or observing general music classes at this level. We struggled to define common terms and make suggestions for providing quality instruction until we realized that part of the problem was the lack of a common definition and understanding of expected learning outcomes for these students. This led us to formulate the following as essential organizing ideas for our discussion:

■ What high school general music is and its differences from general music at the elementary and middle levels.

■ What we want the well-educated modern Renaissance person to know about music.

■ What relevance music study has in preparing high school students for the world of tomorrow.

What Is High School General Music and How Is It Different?

The group decided that it was important to define just what high school general music is. We included keyboarding, guitar, composition, recorder, and world-music courses under the broad umbrella of general music. After much debate we concluded that high school general music was a course designed for students who wish to pursue music study for their own personal satisfaction and have little desire to participate in the traditional large music ensembles. We felt that the course content would be most effective if it were built on the culture and community of the students as well as on their past experiences. We recommended that another, more explicative course title be coined. "General Music" gives too little information about what the students will learn, lacks appeal, and, right or wrong, sounds like the same thing students had in elementary school. Some titles we discussed were Comparative Arts; Musical Perspectives; Discovering Music; World Music I, II, and III; Keys to Music; and From Bach to Rock.

Because many of these students may not have had any formal music training since they were in fifth or sixth grade, we recognized that much of the instruction would be recycling the upper elementary curriculum. We felt that the curriculum should be different from elementary and middle level general music in the following ways:

■ It should be less exploratory, more in depth.

■ It should employ age-appropriate, varied teaching strategies.

■ It should be more relevant to student's lives and interests.

■ It should allow more independence for students to pursue their own musical interests.

One of the major problems teachers deal with at this level is the various ability levels of the students—some have been in performance ensembles or studied privately, others have had limited formal instruction, and others may be essentially self-taught. One way to deal with such diversity is to have modules of programmed instruction so that students can independently proceed with their study. Peer teaching and cooperative learning offer excellent means of individualizing instruction and meeting the various ability levels of the students. The use of technology in the classroom is another means of addressing students' learning needs. Organizing instruction around projects such as composing music for specific purposes, writing and producing a musical, writing program notes for a concert, or researching the musical history of their families or community were also suggested as being age appropriate means of varying instruction.

The group concluded that developing a consensus about just what high school general music should be was critical to it becoming more widely taught and accepted by the profession. Better preparation for teaching secondary general music is necessary at the university level and better materials to support instruction are needed. We strongly advocated more meetings such as this one to foster national agreement about the content and nature of instruction at this level, so we can better serve students who are interested in music but do not wish to commit to performance ensembles.

What Do We Want the Well-Educated Modern Renaissance Person to Know about Music?

We would like to see well-educated adults in our communities use their knowledge of music. The image of the modern Renaissance person was appealing to us, so we then discussed how we would want to see that person use music in daily life. We agreed on these qualities or skills that modern, cultured adults should exhibit:

■ First and foremost they should value all kinds of music.

■ They should be advocates for the arts within their communities.

■ They should possess at least one musical performance skill to employ alone or with others, whether it be singing in church, playing guitar, or performing in a local band or orchestra.

■ They should continue to be curious about music and be lifelong music learners so that they are well-informed music consumers.

■ They need to be aware of the music resources in their communities and know where and how to get information about music.

Finally, we want modern, cultured adults to be curious about new musical ideas and willing to try new music experiences. We felt that they would be people who seek to have music experiences just about every day and who have personal criteria for the music they enjoy and choose to listen to and participate in. They would be active listeners and would use their personal resources of time, finances, and energy to participate in and support music making in the community.

Once we decided what we wanted adults to know about music, we felt that the next logical step was to base the secondary general music curriculum on that knowledge. If, as stated above, we want them to be aware of the music resources in their community, then learning how to identify those resources should be a part of our course of study. If we want them to be advocates for music in the community, then we must make them aware of the people, places, and circumstances where advocacy is needed and how it is done. If we want them to be curious about new music experiences, we need to give them various opportunities to hear and make

music that is different from what they may have done in the past. If we plan our curriculum this way, then the issues of relevance and application in our daily lives begin to be taken care of.

What Is the Relevance of Music Study in Preparing Students for the World of Tomorrow?

We have entered a new age of educational reform that has been primarily directed by forces outside of education. The impact of the SCANS (Secretary's Commission on Achieving Necessary Skills) Report from the Department of Labor has been tremendous. In essence the report outlined the skills students need to have to be successful in the work force of tomorrow. The business world, state legislatures, parents, and students themselves are beginning to ask, "Why do I need to learn this? What good will it do me?" Although the report clearly states that many skills are needed to be successful in life and to be a well-rounded human being, many have looked to SCANS as the new defining force for curriculum development in the age of new reform. Concurrent with this is the research in the area of learning theory that shows that students best retain information and skills that seem relevant to their needs, lives, and interests. Because all the arts are so quickly judged as frills, particularly in times of limited resources, the issue of what is relevant about music study to everyday life is one that should be addressed by all music teachers.

We particularly felt the need to discuss the practical, relevant nature of music study because the students are so soon going into the work force. The following are the life skills that music study fosters:

■ Critical judgment
■ Divergent thinking
■ Dealing with ambiguity
■ Understanding of a basic mode of communication
■ Cooperation
■ Being a team player
■ Self-discipline

- Perseverance
- Problem-solving
- Use of technology
- Sensitivity to others and their environment
- Ties to one's own past or history and that of others
- Knowledge of one's culture and the desire to learn about that of others.

When discussing relevance, it is easy to succumb to the idea that the music styles studied will primarily be those of the contemporary or popular genres. The group strongly felt that this should not be the case. It may be easier for students to see the impact of music from other eras on styles, politics, and entertainment. The need to make general music relevant does not negate the need to make it historically comprehensive. We also discussed, however, the importance of making students aware of the effective use of music in the media and to raise each student's consciousness level about how music can be used by the media to manipulate decision making.

We felt that the practical nature of studying music had long been overlooked by those outside of music education. We also felt that caution was necessary when pursuing this line of reasoning with those who have had limited experience with the arts. Justifying music programs because they teach students to manage their time or to work with others is pushing the secondary benefits of music study and not the primary ones.

Conclusions

Three overall recommendations for improvement of the status of general music at the high school level were generated by the group. The first was the recognition by the profession of the need for diversification of the high school music curriculum. With the changes occurring at the high school level—block scheduling, flexible scheduling, integrated learning, outcome-based instruction, continuous learning progress, and on and on and on—the wave of the future for music education may be general music instruction. With more students committed to afterschool jobs, fewer students are joining traditional large-ensemble programs because of the time commitment for afterschool practices and weekend travel. Diversifying music offerings may be what is needed to attract a whole new group of students.

The second recommendation was that teachers be better prepared to teach the general-music student at the high school level. University teacher preparation programs should at the very least prepare young teachers to teach keyboarding and guitar, introduce them to MIDI and computer-assisted instruction, teach alternative instructional strategies such as peer coaching and cooperative learning, and make them aware of the world of music outside of the band, chorus, and orchestra programs. We need to prepare new teachers and assist experienced teachers for teaching in the world of tomorrow.

For over half of our population, high school will be the last opportunity they have to receive formal music instruction. These may be our future school board members, legislators, parents, advocates, or detractors. If we truly believe that music is for everyone, then we need to go about the business of making our belief a reality. Developing a nationwide consensus about the nature and purpose of general music at the high school level may grow out of the National Standards effort. Our final recommendation was that MENC continue to support regional and national meetings that will help develop such a consensus.

The discussion group lead by David Myers and Chelcy Bowles addressed a diverse array of issues and constituencies as they considered the changing roles of college and community music educators. Their conversations focused on college course offerings for music majors as well as teachers of other subjects and students majoring in fields outside music, on the transition from music student to music teacher, on the needs of the nonprofessional adult music learner, and on connections to the community. The recommendations provide an agenda for general music education that heeds the emphasis growing worldwide for education throughout life.

General Music Education
College through Adulthood

By David Myers and Chelcy Bowles

Complex thinking, creative problem solving, and humanistic valuing are cited repeatedly as essential educational outcomes for citizens of the twenty-first century. Music and arts education can figure significantly in attaining these goals. At all ages and levels, however, music learning too often is considered peripheral, rather than central, to the knowledge and skills most closely allied with successful living.

General music educators thus face a continuing challenge to link music learning with broad educational aims. In addition, they must demonstrate the relevance of music learning to living not only more productively, but also with compassion and sensitivity in a global society. What role do college and community music educators play in strengthening music learning opportunities for "general" students of all ages in the twenty-first century? As participants in the Reflections and Applications group raised diverse issues and considered possible recommendations, several themes emerged. Among these were the following:

David Myers is associate professor of music at Georgia State University School of Music, and Chelcy Bowles is assistant professor of music at University of Wisconsin–Madison.

■ Music education in schools and communities should relate more directly to the music experiences students have beyond school, particularly those closely tied to family, ethnic, and cultural traditions and values.

■ The population of college students is continually changing. Increasingly, students in higher education represent greater diversity in age, ethnic and cultural background, and experiences. Some may bring sophisticated knowledge of certain kinds of music.

■ Lifelong learning can be a unifying construct for general music education. Career patterns in the twenty-first century will involve several changes over the course of adult life. Important challenges and opportunities will arise with predicted developments, such as stronger connections among preschool, K–12, college, and adult education; a growing older-adult population; and increasing worldwide emphasis on education throughout life. These developments offer important challenges and opportunities for music educators.

■ Technology offers untold opportunities for improved creativity in learning, as well as connectedness among students, teachers, and programs around the globe. Technology, however, may also threaten the uniquely personal and social dimensions of music learning and music making. General music educators can be at the forefront of ensuring appropriate implementation of technology in music education.

■ The developmental needs of students of all ages, including college students and adults, are an important element of program development. Increased understanding of reasons for continued music participation, as well as reasons for nonparticipation, can help guide general music instruction both in and beyond traditional school settings.

Discussion Topics and Recommendations. To focus its discussions, the College and Continuing Education group initially defined four major topic areas: 1) teaching/learning process, or "methods," courses in general music, including those for music education majors and those designed primarily for teachers of other subject areas; 2) the transition from music student to music teacher; 3) education needs of the nonprofessional adult music learner; and 4) college/university "service" courses—those music courses intended to satisfy general education requirements of students majoring in fields outside of music.

General Music Learning/Teaching Courses (Methods)

Suggestions for setting goals and adopting criteria for music education majors were framed in the context of four major thrusts: 1) integration of general music into the total school curriculum and collaboration among music teachers and other subject-area teachers in the school program; 2) emphasis on developing effective teaching skills in general music; 3) increased contact and experiences in the school and community prior to student teaching; 4) research-based knowledge regarding the importance of music learning in the total educational program. These general aims, combined with concerns and predictions suggested by the major conference speakers, led toward the following recommendations:

■ Provide concrete examples and practice in integrating general music with subjects and themes across the curriculum.

■ Provide techniques for establishing the faculty as integral within the school.

■ Emphasize communication skills for relating intellectually and socially with non–music teaching colleagues.

■ Strengthen knowledge and skills in teaching students, as well as teaching the subject.

■ Ensure that preservice teachers develop practical skills for managing classrooms.

■ Stress the importance of teaching as a profession.

■ Emphasize the responsibility of the music teacher to be prepared to teach students of all age levels.

■ Encourage consideration of opportunities to meet the musical needs of colleagues in other subject areas as a part of the music teacher's role.

■ Increase and present research-based knowledge of the importance of music learning in intellectual, as well as affective and aesthetic, development.

■ Present and facilitate greater research-based knowledge regarding the role of music learning in developing extramusical knowledge and skills.

■ Ensure knowledge of, and experience with, current technological trends, materials, and equipment.

■ Ensure adequate opportunities for interaction with young students in school or lab settings prior to student teaching.

■ Consider establishing shared teaching responsibilities among K–12 and higher-education music faculties.

Courses for Teachers of Other Subjects

Traditionally, these courses serve preservice elementary classroom teachers; however, changes in teacher education programs are resulting in graduate-level courses for experienced teachers, as well as courses for individuals with degrees who are seeking a teaching certificate. Some colleges offer integrated arts courses to assist secondary-level humanities faculty in teaching elective courses that include music learning. Projected trends suggest that education and career patterns of the twenty-first century may broaden the audience for these courses.

The consensus of the discussion in this group was that classroom teachers may play a critical role in students' views of music, including attitude toward music class, assumptions that music is equal in value to other subjects, and applications of music learning beyond the music classroom. Classroom teachers should be prepared to foster positive attitudes toward music as a basic component of education. They also should understand and visibly support the music program, provide experiences with music that help teach concepts and knowledge across the curriculum, and suggest experiences for musical development outside of school.

College music educators who teach classroom teachers may be concerned largely with alleviating music anxiety and with providing experiences that relate to extramusical, as well as musical, objectives for their students. Important methods experiences and assignments are those that provide positive musical and educational experiences, increased knowledge of the role of music in human development, and strategies for incorporating music in the teaching of extramusical concepts and skills. Specific recommendations included the following:

■ Deemphasize assessment of musical skill development as an end; instead, offer low-risk skill development experiences that foster comfort with music participation.

■ Discover and build on prior levels of music experience and achievement and suggest avenues of continued music participation.

■ Focus on skills for engaging students in musical behaviors; that is, creating, performing, listening, and moving rather than learning about music.

■ Provide research-based knowledge of the importance of music in human development.

■ Provide research-based knowledge of the relevance of music experiences and learning to academic and social objectives.

■ Provide practice in incorporating music into the teaching of other subjects.

■ Offer activities that integrate music into classroom routines; for example, cues for directives, background for other activities, exercise, and pacing.

■ Provide music learning and participation experiences that reflect actual school experiences to enhance prospective teachers' understanding of the purpose and scope of the general music program.

The Transition from Music Student to Music Teacher

Discussions under this topic dealt with issues of fluidity between the college experience and the initial teaching job. The following recommendations reflect concern with the nature and quality of collegiate preparation for teaching, and with support mechanisms for beginning teachers.

College and classroom experiences:

■ Be stringent in ensuring that students accepted into music education programs possess the requisite qualities for becoming professional music educators.

■ Maintain open channels of information and communication among music education majors, particularly to enhance understanding of professional opportunities and responsibilities beyond the scope of methods courses.

■ Increase opportunities for interaction between college teacher education students and students in K–12 school and community settings.

■ Provide informal associations between college students and professional teachers through social events, observations, and workshops.

■ Endeavor to build apprenticeship opportunities with adequate economic and professional support.

■ Use problem-solving assignments and strategies that reflect true classroom situations across a variety of responsibilities—instructional, management, collegial, and parental.

■ Encourage reflective thinking as a basis for moving from "musician as teacher" to "teacher as musician."

■ Instill lifelong learning as an important trait of teachers; encourage the development of a personal library of materials and resources.

■ Model interdisciplinary and integrative teaching and learning, technology exploration, problem solving, research implementation, and instruction strategies for learners of all ages.

Support mechanisms for beginning teachers:

■ Encourage and help develop networks of colleagues who are new teachers.

■ Work to develop networks of experienced teachers and college-level instructors; both groups can assist beginning teachers.

■ Make full use of e-mail, fax, and other electronic networking systems for maintaining contacts with beginning teachers, setting up support opportunities in new geographic areas, and responding to teachers' questions and concerns.

■ Provide a crisis line for instructional emergencies.

■ Assist new teachers in evaluating teaching via videotaped lessons.

■ Work toward a continuum of professional development opportunities that keep teachers abreast of current knowledge and foster communication regarding problems and successes of the beginning teaching experience.

The Nonprofessional Adult Music Learner

The continuation of music learning through adulthood is a concern both for traditional school-based music educators and for those endeavoring to provide community-based adult programs. While some adults possess sufficient confidence and skill to participate in church and community performing groups or to attend music appreciation classes, many adults who are interested in music refrain from such opportunities. There is a need to bridge the gap between public school programs and adult education in music by providing instruction for adults at all levels of music confidence, understanding, and experience. In addition, it must be recognized that adulthood includes an age range representing major developmental evolution, and that

music learning experiences need to be tailored to the intellectual, psychosocial, and physical changes that occur with increasing years. Recommendations from this discussion to the profession include the following:

■ Work to provide music-learning opportunities at all levels of understanding and achievement across the life span.

■ Advance and support development of music education careers that link schools and communities in a music-learning continuum. Music educators can aid in personal and community development through working with housing authorities, recreation programs, apartment and condominium services, business and industry education programs, community schools, and older-adult services.

■ Provide opportunities for music education majors to teach a variety of age groups, including adults, in both formal and informal settings and in cross-generational and crosscultural contexts.

■ Incorporate into professional music education courses knowledge and experience with program planning, adult development and learning, and methods for adult learners.

■ Provide opportunities for music education majors to be more affirming of the music experiences and knowledge students bring from families and communities and to develop strategies for relating school music more closely with music experiences beyond the school walls. These strategies may involve increased familiarity and connections with performers, performance venues, and music opportunities representing diverse cultural and ethnic experiences.

■ Encourage music educators to become model learners, in which teaching and learning are integrated processes; demonstrate opportunities and values associated with lifelong music learning and participation.

■ Increase opportunities for adults and older adults to enroll in college-level music courses and encourage music educators to design and implement courses for programs such as Elderhostel.

College Music Courses in General Education

Discussions under this topic led toward a consensus that music courses for the nonmajor are an important component of general music education. Because they provide opportunities for nonprofessional music learners to understand and value the experience of music, they are integral to the goal of developing a musically literate society. Among the recommendations for teaching these courses were the following:

■ Provide experiences with sophisticated music behaviors and thinking through basic skills.

■ Emphasize music making, participation, and perceptive listening.

■ Foster skill development that can be extended on a personal basis.

■ Stress course experiences that are relevant to the experiences, interests, and backgrounds of students; give specific ideas and assignments that demonstrate applications of learning beyond the classroom.

■ Instill lifelong music learning as a goal by providing specific avenues by which the student may pursue lifelong music learning; for example, skills with folk instruments, basic reading skills, focused listening skills, and assignments involving self-direction skills.

■ Emphasize music as a vehicle for expression of social concerns and as an important element of ethnic and cultural heritage and interaction. Teaching should relate music to contemporary issues such as cultural pluralism, gender and racial concerns, environmental considerations, and so on.

■ Include exploration of music technology as a component of classes for the general student.

■ Assign professors with expertise in learning and teaching music to courses for the general student.

Conclusion

These recommendations suggest possible components of an agenda for general music in the twenty-first century. The discussions that led toward these recommendations featured lively interchange and a keen interest among participants in exploring the issues further. The renewed energy everyone felt as a result of this sharing is in itself a significant step toward realizing our goals.

Related MENC Publications

Elementary General Music: The Best of MEJ. A set of effective how-to ideas for elementary general music teachers from the pages of the *Music Educators Journal.* Edited by Betty W. Atterbury. 1992. 136 pages. ISBN 1-56545-013-2. MENC stock #1613.

Promising Practices: High School General Music. An examination of ten innovative programs. Includes sample lesson plans and presents practical considerations involved in managing each program examined. Edited by Mary Palmer. 1989. 112 pages. ISBN 0-940796-65-1. MENC stock #1499.

Singing in General Music. On video from MENC's Society for General Music, a discussion of the importance of singing in general music from noted vocal experts and demonstrations of techniques for teaching singing. 1994. VHS. 26 minutes. ISBN 1-56545-047-7. MENC stock #3082.

Teaching General Music: A Course of Study. A model for developing a strong program of instruction for teaching general music from preschool to high school. Developed by the MENC Task Force on General Music Course of Study. 1991. 40 pages. ISBN 0-940796-98-8. MENC stock #1602.

Standards Publications

National Standards for Arts Education: What Every Young American Should Know and Be Able to Do in the Arts. Content and achievement standards for music, dance, theatre, and visual arts for grades K–12. Developed by the Consortium of National Arts Education Associations under the guidance of the National Committee for Standards in the Arts. 1994. 148 pages. ISBN 1-56545-036-1. MENC stock #1605.

Opportunity-to-Learn Standards for Music Instruction. Recommends the conditions schools should provide in order to achieve both the National Standards for Music Education in grades K–12 and the MENC standards for music education in prekindergarten. 1994. 32 pages. ISBN 1-56545-040-X. MENC stock #1619.

The School Music Program: A New Vision. The K–12 National Music Standards and MENC prekindergarten standards. 1994. 48 pages. ISBN 1-56545-039-6. MENC stock #1618.

Teaching Examples: Ideas for Music Educators. A collection of sample instructional strategies to help teachers design and implement a curriculum leading to achievement of the standards. Project Director: Paul R. Lehman. 1994. 142 pages. ISBN 1-56545-041-8. MENC Stock #1620.

For information on these and other MENC publications, write to:

MENC Publications Sales
1806 Robert Fulton Drive
Reston, VA 22091-4348
Credit card holders may call 800-828-0229.